CHRONOLOGICAL TABLES FOR SOUTHERN INDIA

FROM THE SIXTH CENTURY A.D.

CHRONOLOGICAL TABLES
FOR
SOUTHERN INDIA

FROM THE SIXTH CENTURY A.D.

BY

ROBERT SEWELL,

Madras Civil Service.

GYAN

Published by

Gyan Publishing House
5, Ansari Road
Daryaganj, New Delhi-110002
Phone: 011-47034999, 9811692060
E-mail: books@gyanbooks.com

Distribution Network
gyanbooks.com
India, USA, Canada, UK, Australia, France

ISBN : 978-81-212-2164-1 (HB)
First Published, 1881

2nd Impression 2021

Printed at: Gyan Press, Delhi.

Chronological Tables for Southern India
Author: Robert Sewell

CHRONOLOGICAL TABLES

FOR

SOUTHERN INDIA

FROM THE SIXTH CENTURY A.D.

BY

ROBERT SEWELL,
MADRAS CIVIL SERVICE.

Printed by Authority.

MADRAS:
PRINTED BY E. KEYS, AT THE GOVERNMENT PRESS.
1881.

CHRONOLOGICAL TABLES.

THESE Tables are published in order to enable those at work on the Inscriptions of Southern India readily to ascertain the date of any document, or record on stone. The *Śālivāhana Śaka* era being the one most commonly used, it is placed in the first column. The *Kaliyuga* era is very commonly inserted in addition to the first, especially in the later inscriptions. The *Kollaṁ* era of Quilon is only used in the Southern Tamil country and in Travancore. The name of the cyclic year occurs in almost all the inscriptions of Southern India since the tenth century. The year of the *Hijra* is only used in Muhammadan inscriptions. Burnell's "*South Indian Palæography*" (pp. 70—80) contains some very useful notes on the eras in use in the Madras Presidency. Prinsep's "Indian Chronological Tables," in Thomas's edition of the former's "*Indian Antiquities*" (Vol. II, pp. 131—214), constitute the most critically accurate information yet published on the subject. And Cowasjee Patell's "*Chronology*" (London: Trübner and Co., 1866) may with advantage be consulted; as well as Brown's "*Cyclic Tables.*"

Taking the *Śaka*, *Kaliyuga*, and cyclic years—which may be considered, for all ordinary purposes, to commence and finish simultaneously—as my base, I have thought it best to approximate the other eras to these, rather than to approximate all eras to the Christian, as is often done. And, since the *Śaka*, *Kaliyuga*, and cyclic years may be considered to commence together about March each year, it follows that the *Kollaṁ Āṇḍu* of Quilon, which commences about September, runs half with one, and half with another of the former years; while the Christian year, commencing in January, runs three-quarters with one, and a quarter with the following of those standard years. Hence I have printed the two *Kollaṁ* years in numerals of the same size, meaning that the *Śaka*, &c., year corresponds to half of one and half of the next years so printed; while the large and small figures of the Christian years mean three-quarters of the first and a quarter of the second. Thus, in the *Śaka* year 938, *Kaliyuga* 4117, cyclic year *Nala*, there were six months (or half) of the *Kollaṁ* year 192, and six (or half) of 193; nine months (or three-quarters) of the Christian year A.D. 1016, and three months (or one-quarter) of A.D. 1017. If this be borne in mind, the difference in size of the figures will materially assist those desirous of ascertaining approximately the correspondence of dates in the different eras. But it must be strictly remembered that, in reality, there will be in every year a few days which vary, and therefore, if great accuracy be required, a far closer calculation must be made. For such purposes Prinsep's Tables will be found to be the most reliable guide.

The *Hijra* year,—commencing July 16th, A.D. 622 (the day following Muhammad's flight to Medina, which took place on the night of Thursday, 15th July),—being a lunar year, is incapable of being approximated to the solar years in a convenient tabular form, and I have therefore inserted in each year the actual day of its commencement in the corresponding Christian era. Where the *Hijra* date is given in an inscription it would be very rare to find any other era referred to, and therefore it seemed needless to make any tabular approximation between the Muhammadan and Indian systems.

ROBERT SEWELL,
Madras Civil Service.

Year of the *Sálivâhana Śaka*.	Year of the *Kaliyuga*.	Cyclic Year.	*Kollam Āṇḍu*, or Era of Quilon.	Christian Era (A.D.)	The *Hijra* Year commences.
500	3679	Vilambi	.. ..	578—579	
501	3680	Vikāri	.. ..	579—580	
502	3681	Śarvari	.. ..	580—581	
503	3682	Plava	.. ..	581—582	
504	3683	Śubhakṛit ..	.. ..	582—583	
505	3684	Śobhana, or -kṛit.	.. ..	583—584	
506	3685	Krodhi	.. ..	584—585	
507	3686	Viśvāvasu ..	.. ..	585—586	
508	3687	Parābhava ..	.. ..	586—587	
509	3688	Plavaṅga ..	.. ..	587—588	
510	3689	Kīlaka	.. ..	588—589	
511	3690	Saumya	.. ..	589—590	
512	3691	Sādhāraṇa ..	.. ..	590—591	
513	3692	Virodhikṛit ..	.. ..	591—592	
514	3693	Parīdhāvi, or -pi.	.. ..	592—593	
515	3694	Pramādīcha ..	.. ..	593—594	
516	3695	Ānanda	.. ..	594—595	
517	3696	Rākshasa ..	.. ..	595—596	
518	3697	Nala	.. ..	596—597	
519	3698	Piṅgala	.. ..	597—598	
520	3699	Kālayukti ..	.. ..	598—599	
521	3700	Siddhārthi ..	.. ..	599—600	
522	3701	Raudri	.. ..	600—601	
523	3702	Durmati	.. ..	601—602	
524	3703	Dundubhi ..	.. ..	602—603	
525	3704	Rudhirodgāri ..	.. ..	603—604	
526	3705	Raktākshi ..	.. ..	604—605	
527	3706	Krodhana ..	.. ..	605—606	
528	3707	Akshaya	.. ..	606—607	
529	3708	Prabhava ..	.. ..	607—608	
530	3709	Vibhava	.. ..	608—609	
531	3710	Śukla	.. ..	609—610	
532	3711	Pramodūta ..	.. ..	610—611	
533	3712	Prajotpatti ..	.. ..	611—612	
534	3713	Āṅgirasa ..	.. ..	612—613	
535	3714	Śrīmukha ..	.. ..	613—614	
536	3715	Bhava	.. ..	614—615	
537	3716	Yuva	.. ..	615—616	
538	3717	Dhātu	.. ..	616—617	

Year of the *Śālivāhana Śaka*.	Year of the *Kaliyuga*.	Cyclic Year.	*Kollam Āndu*, or Era of Quilon.	Christian Era (A.D.)	The *Hijra* Year commences.
539	3718	Īśvara	.. ..	617 – 618	
540	3719	Bahudhānya ..	.. ..	618 – 619	
541	3720	Pramādhi ..	.. ..	619 – 620	
542	3721	Vikrama	.. ..	620 – 621	
543	3722	Vishu, or Vṛishu ..	.. ..	621 – 622	
544	3723	Chitrabhānu ..	.. ..	622 – 623	1. July 16, 622.
545	3724	Subhānu	.. ..	623 – 624	2. July 5, 623.
546	3725	Tāraṇa	.. ..	624 – 625	3. June 24, 624.
547	3726	Pārthiva	.. ..	625 – 626	4. June 13, 625.
548	3727	Vyaya	.. ..	626 – 627	5. June 2, 626.
549	3728	Sarvajit	.. ..	627 – 628	6. May 23, 627.
550	3729	Sarvadhāri ..	.. ..	628 – 629	7. May 11, 628.
551	3730	Virodhi	.. ..	629 – 630	8. May 1, 629.
552	3731	Vikṛiti	.. ..	630 – 631	9. April 20, 630.
553	3732	Khara	.. ..	631 – 632	10. April 9, 631.
554	3733	Nandana ..	.. ..	632 – 633	11. March 29, 632.
555	3734	Vijaya	.. ..	633 – 634	12. March 18, 633.
556	3735	Jaya	.. ..	634 – 635	13. March 7, 634.
557	3736	Manmadha ..	.. ..	635 – 636	14. Feb. 25, 635.
558	3737	Durmukhi ..	.. ..	636 – 637	15. Feb. 14, 636.
559	3738	Hevilaṁbi ..	.. ..	637 – 638	16. Feb. 2, 637.
560	3739	Vilaṁbi	.. ..	638 – 639	17. Jan. 23, 638.
561	3740	Vikāri	.. ..	639 – 640	18. Jan. 12, 639. 19. Dec. 31, 639.
562	3741	Śārvari	.. ..	640 – 641	20. Dec. 21, 640.
563	3742	Plava	.. ..	641 – 642	21. Dec. 10, 641.
564	3743	Śubhakṛit ..	.. ..	642 – 643	22. Nov. 30, 642.
565	3744	Śobhana, or -kṛit.	.. ..	643 – 644	23. Nov. 19, 643.
566	3745	Krodhi	.. ..	644 – 645	24. Nov. 7, 644.
567	3746	Viśvāvasu ..	.. ..	645 – 646	25. Oct. 28, 645.
568	3747	Parābhava ..	.. ..	646 – 647	26. Oct. 17, 646.
569	3748	Plavaṅga ..	.. ..	647 – 648	27. Oct. 7, 647.
570	3749	Kīlaka	.. ..	648 – 649	28. Sept. 25, 648.
571	3750	Saumya	.. ..	649 – 650	29. Sept. 14, 649.
572	3751	Sādhāraṇa ..	.. ..	650 – 651	30. Sept. 4, 650.
573	3752	Virodhikṛit ..	.. ..	651 – 652	31. Aug. 24, 651.
574	3753	Parīdhāvi, or -pi ..	.. ..	652 – 653	32. Aug. 12, 652.
575	3754	Pramādīcha ..	.. ..	653 – 654	33. Aug. 2, 653.
576	3755	Ānanda	.. ..	654 – 655	34. July 22, 654.

Year of the *Śâlivâhana Śaka*.	Year of the *Kaliyuga*.	Cyclic Year.	*Kollam Āndu*, or Era of Quilon.	Christian Era (A.D.)	The *Hijra* Year commences.
577	3756	Rākshasa ..	.. ..	655 – 656	35. July 11, 655.
578	3757	Nala	.. ..	656 – 657	36. June 30, 656.
579	3758	Piṅgala	.. ..	657 – 658	37. June 19, 657.
580	3759	Kālayukti ..	.. ..	658 – 659	38. June 9, 658.
581	3760	Siddhārthi ..	.. ..	659 – 660	39. May 29, 659.
582	3761	Raudri	.. ..	660 – 661	40. May 17, 660.
583	3762	Durmati	.. ..	661 – 662	41. May 7, 661.
584	3763	Dundubhi ..	.. ..	662 – 663	42. April 26, 662.
585	3764	Rudhirodgāri ..	.. ..	663 – 664	43. April 15, 663.
586	3765	Raktākshi ..	.. ..	664 – 665	44. April 4, 664.
587	3766	Krodhana ..	.. ..	665 – 666	45. March 24, 665.
588	3767	Akshaya	.. ..	666 – 667	46. March 13, 666.
589	3768	Prabhava ..	.. ..	667 – 668	47. March 3, 667.
590	3769	Vibhava	.. ..	668 – 669	48. Feb. 20, 668.
591	3770	Śukla	.. ..	669 – 670	49. Feb. 9, 669.
592	3771	Pramodūta ..	.. ..	670 – 671	50. Jan. 29, 670.
593	3772	Prajotpatti ..	.. ..	671 – 672	51. Jan. 18, 671.
594	3773	Āṅgirasa ..	.. ..	672 – 673	52. Jan. 8, 672. 53. Dec. 27, 672.
595	3774	Śrīmukha ..	.. ..	673 – 674	54. Dec. 16. 673.
596	3775	Bhava	.. ..	674 – 675	55. Dec. 6, 674.
597	3776	Yuva	.. ..	675 – 676	56. Nov. 25, 675.
598	3777	Dhātu	.. ..	676 – 677	57. Nov. 14, 676.
599	3778	Īśvara	.. ..	677 – 678	58. Nov. 3, 677.
600	3779	Bahudhānya ..	.. ..	678 – 679	59. Oct. 23, 678.
601	3780	Pramādhi ..	.. ..	679 – 680	60. Oct. 13, 679.
602	3781	Vikrama	.. ..	680 – 681	61. Oct. 1, 680.
603	3782	Vishu, or Vṛishu ..	.. ..	681 – 682	62. Sept. 20, 681.
604	3783	Chitrabhānu ..	.. ..	682 – 683	63. Sept. 10. 682.
605	3784	Subhānu	.. ..	683 – 684	64. Aug. 30, 683.
606	3785	Tāraṇa	.. ..	684 – 685	65. Aug. 18, 684.
607	3786	Pārthiva	.. ..	685 – 686	66. Aug. 8, 685.
608	3787	Vyaya	.. ..	686 – 687	67. July 28, 686.
609	3788	Sarvajit	.. ..	687 – 688	68. July 18, 687.
610	3789	Sarvadhāri ..	.. ..	688 – 689	69. July 6, 688.
611	3790	Virodhi	.. ..	689 – 690	70. June 25, 689.
612	3791	Vikṛiti	.. ..	690 – 691	71. June 15, 690.
613	3792	Khara	.. ..	691 – 692	72. June 4, 691.
614	3793	Nandana ..	.. ..	692 – 693	73. May 23, 692.

Year of the *Śālivāhana Śaka.*	Year of the *Kaliyuga.*	Cyclic Year.	*Kollam Āṇḍu*, or Era of Quilon.	Christian Era (A.D.)	The *Hijra* Year commences.
615	3794	Vijaya	.. ..	693 – 694	74. May 13, 693.
616	3795	Jaya	.. ..	694 – 695	75. May 2, 694.
617	3796	Manmadha ..	.. ..	695 – 696	76. April 21, 695.
618	3797	Durmukhi ..	.. ..	696 – 697	77. April 10, 696.
619	3798	Hevilaṁbi ..	.. ..	697 – 698	78. March 30, 697.
620	3799	Vilaṁbi	.. ..	698 – 699	79. March 20, 698.
621	3800	Vikāri	.. ..	699 – 700	80. March 9, 699.
622	3801	Śārvari	.. ..	700 – 701	81. Feb. 26, 700.
623	3802	Plava	.. ..	701 – 702	82. Feb. 15, 701.
624	3803	Śubhakṛit ..	.. ..	702 – 703	83. Feb. 4, 702.
625	3804	Śobhana, or -kṛit.	.. ..	703 – 704	84. Jan. 24, 703.
626	3805	Krodhi	.. ..	704 – 705	85. Jan. 14, 704.
627	3806	Viśvāvasu ..	..	705 – 706	86. Jan. 2, 705. 87. Dec. 23, 705.
628	3807	Parābhava ..	.. ..	706 – 707	88. Dec. 12, 706.
629	3808	Plavaṅga ..	.. ..	707 – 708	89. Dec. 1, 707.
630	3809	Kīlaka	.. ..	708 – 709	90. Nov. 20, 708.
631	3810	Saumya	.. ..	709 – 710	91. Nov. 9, 709.
632	3811	Sādhāraṇa ..	.. ..	710 – 711	92. Oct. 29, 710.
633	3812	Virodhikṛit ..	.. ..	711 – 712	93. Oct. 19, 711.
634	3813	Parīdhāvi, or -pi.	.. ..	712 – 713	94. Oct. 7, 712.
635	3814	Pramādīcha ..	.. ..	713 – 714	95. Sept. 26, 713.
636	3815	Ānanda	.. ..	714 – 715	96. Sept. 16, 714.
637	3816	Rākshasa ..	.. ..	715 – 716	97. Sept. 5, 715.
638	3817	Nala	.. ..	716 – 717	98. Aug. 25, 716.
639	3818	Piṅgala	.. ..	717 – 718	99. Aug. 14, 717.
640	3819	Kālayukti ..	.. ..	718 – 719	100. Aug. 3, 718.
641	3820	Siddhārthi ..	.. ..	719 – 720	101. July 24, 719.
642	3821	Raudri	.. ..	720 – 721	102. July 12, 720.
643	3822	Durmati	.. ..	721 – 722	103. July 1, 721.
644	3823	Dundubhi ..	.. ..	722 – 723	104. June 21, 722.
645	3824	Rudhirodgāri ..	.. ..	723 – 724	105. June 10, 723.
646	3825	Raktākshi ..	.. ..	724 – 725	106. May 29, 724.
647	3826	Krodhana ..	.. ..	725 – 726	107. May 19, 725.
648	3827	Akshaya	.. ..	726 – 727	108. May 8, 726.
649	3828	Prabhava ..	.. ..	727 – 728	109. April 28, 727.
650	3829	Vibhava	.. ..	728 – 729	110. April 16, 728.
651	3830	Śukla	.. ..	729 – 730	111. April 5, 729.
652	3831	Pramodūta ..	.. ..	730 – 731	112. March 26, 730.

Year of the *Śālivāhana Śaka*.	Year of the *Kaliyuga*.	Cyclic Year.	*Kollam Āndu*, or Era of Quilon.	Christian Era (A.D.)	The *Hijra* Year commences.
653	3832	Prajotpatti ..	.. ..	731 – 732	113. March 15, 731.
654	3833	Āṅgirasa ..	.. ..	732 – 733	114. March 3, 732.
655	3834	Śrīmukha ..	.. ..	733 – 734	115. Feb. 21, 733.
656	3835	Bhava	.. ..	734 – 735	116. Feb. 10, 734.
657	3836	Yuva	.. ..	735 – 736	117. Jan. 31, 735.
658	3837	Dhātu	.. ..	736 – 737	118. Jan. 20, 736.
659	3838	Īśvara	.. ..	787 – 738	119. Jan. 8, 737. 120. Dec. 29, 737.
660	3839	Bahudhānya ..	.. ..	738 – 739	121. Dec. 18, 738.
661	3840	Pramādhi ..	.. ..	739 – 740	122. Dec. 7, 739.
662	3841	Vikrama	.. ..	740 – 741	123. Nov. 26, 740.
663	3842	Vishu, or Vṛishu.	.. ..	741 – 742	124. Nov. 15, 741.
664	3843	Chitrabhānu ..	.. ..	742 – 743	125. Nov. 4, 742.
665	3844	Subhānu	.. ..	743 – 744	126. Oct. 25, 743.
666	3845	Tāraṇa	.. ..	744 – 745	127. Oct. 13, 744.
667	3846	Pārthiva	.. ..	745 – 746	128. Oct. 3, 745.
668	3847	Vyaya	.. ..	746 – 747	129. Sept. 22, 746.
669	3848	Sarvajit	.. ..	747 – 748	130. Sept. 11, 747.
670	3849	Sarvadhāri ..	.. ..	748 – 749	131. Aug. 31, 748.
671	3850	Virodhi	.. ..	749 – 750	132. Aug. 20, 749.
672	3851	Vikṛiti	.. ..	750 – 751	133. Aug. 9, 750.
673	3852	Khara	.. ..	751 – 752	134. July 30, 751.
674	3853	Nandana ..	.. ..	752 – 753	135. July 18, 752.
675	3854	Vijaya	.. ..	753 – 754	136. July 7, 753.
676	3855	Jaya	.. ..	754 – 755	137. June 27, 754.
677	3856	Manmadha ..	.. ..	755 – 756	138. June 16, 755.
678	3857	Durmukhi ..	.. ..	756 – 757	139. June 5, 756.
679	3858	Hevilaṁbi ..	.. ..	757 – 758	140. May 25, 757.
680	3859	Vilaṁbi	.. ..	758 – 759	141. May 14, 758.
681	3860	Vikāri	.. ..	759 – 760	142. May 4, 759.
682	3861	Śārvari	.. ..	760 – 761	143. April 22, 760.
683	3862	Plava	.. ..	761 – 762	144. April 11, 761.
684	3863	Śubhakṛit ..	.. ..	762 – 763	145. April 1, 762.
685	3864	Śobhana, or -kṛit.	.. ..	763 – 764	146. March 21, 763.
686	3865	Krodhi	.. ..	764 – 765	147. March 10, 764.
687	3866	Viśvāvasu ..	.. ..	765 – 766	148. Feb. 27, 765.
688	3867	Parābhava ..	.. ..	766 – 767	149. Feb. 16, 766.
689	3868	Plavaṅga ..	.. ..	767 – 768	150. Feb. 6, 767.
690	3869	Kīlaka	.. ..	768 – 769	151. Jan. 26, 768.

Year of the *Śālivāhana Śaka.*	Year of the *Kaliyuga.*	Cyclic Year.	*Kollam Āndu*, or Era of Quilon.	Christian Era (A.D.)	The *Hijra* Year commences.
691	3870	Saumya	.. ..	769 – 770	152. Jan. 14, 769.
692	3871	Sādhāraṇa ..	.. ..	770 – 771	153. Jan. 4, 770. 154. Dec. 24, 770.
693	3872	Virodhikṛit ..	.. ..	771 – 772	155. Dec. 13, 771.
694	3873	Parīdhāvi, or -pi.	.. ..	772 – 773	156. Dec. 2, 772.
695	3874	Pramādīcha ..	.. ..	773 – 774	157. Nov. 21, 773.
696	3875	Ānanda	.. ..	774 – 775	158. Nov. 11, 774.
697	3876	Rākshasa ..	.. ..	775 – 776	159. Oct. 31, 775.
698	3877	Nala	.. ..	776 – 777	160. Oct. 19, 776.
699	3878	Piṅgala	.. ..	777 – 778	161. Oct. 9, 777.
700	3879	Kālayukti ..	.. ..	778 – 779	162. Sept. 28, 778.
701	3880	Siddhārthi ..	.. ..	779 – 780	163. Sept. 17, 779.
702	3881	Raudri	.. ..	780 – 781	164. Sept. 6, 780.
703	3882	Durmati ..	.. ..	781 – 782	165. Aug. 26, 781.
704	3883	Dundubhi ..	.. ..	782 – 783	166. Aug. 15, 782.
705	3884	Rudhirodgāri ..	.. ..	783 – 784	167. Aug. 5, 783.
706	3885	Raktākshi ..	.. ..	784 – 785	168. July 24, 784.
707	3886	Krodhana ..	.. ..	785 – 786	169. July 14, 785.
708	3887	Akshaya	.. ..	786 – 787	170. July 3, 786.
709	3888	Prabhava ..	.. ..	787 – 788	171. June 22, 787.
710	3889	Vibhava ..	.. ..	788 – 789	172. June 11, 788.
711	3890	Śukla	.. ..	789 – 790	173. May 31, 789.
712	3891	Pramodūta ..	.. ..	790 – 791	174. May 20, 790.
713	3892	Prajotpatti ..	.. ..	791 – 792	175. May 10, 791.
714	3893	Āṅgirasa ..	.. ..	792 – 793	176. April 28, 792.
715	3894	Śrīmukha ..	.. ..	793 – 794	177. April 18, 793.
716	3895	Bhava	.. ..	794 – 795	178. April 7, 794.
717	3896	Yuva	.. ..	795 – 796	179. March 27, 795.
718	3897	Dhātu	.. ..	796 – 797	180. March 16, 796.
719	3898	Īśvara	.. ..	797 – 798	181. March 5, 797.
720	3899	Bahudhānya ..	.. ..	798 – 799	182. Feb. 22, 798.
721	3900	Pramādhi ..	.. ..	799 – 800	183. Feb. 12, 799.
722	3901	Vikrama ..	.. ..	800 – 801	184. Feb. 1, 800.
723	3902	Vishu, or Vṛishu.	.. ..	801 – 802	185. Jan. 20, 801.
724	3903	Chitrabhānu ..	.. ..	802 – 803	186. Jan. 10, 802.
725	3904	Subhānu ..	.. ..	803 – 804	187. Dec. 30, 802. 188. Dec. 20, 803.
726	3905	Tāraṇa	.. ..	804 – 805	189. Dec. 8, 804.
727	3906	Pārthiva ..	.. ..	805 – 806	190. Nov. 27, 805.

Year of the *Śālivāhana Śaka.*	Year of the *Kaliyuga.*	Cyclic Year.	*Kollam Āṇḍu*, or Era of Quilon.	Christian Era (A.D.)	The *Hijra* Year commences.
728	3907	Vyaya	.. ..	806 – 807	191. Nov. 17, 806.
729	3908	Sarvajit .. .	.. ..	807 – 808	192. Nov. 6, 807.
730	3909	Sarvadhāri ..	.. ..	808 – 809	193. Oct. 25, 808.
731	3910	Virodhi ..	.. ..	809 – 810	194. Oct. 15, 809.
732	3911	Vikṛiti	.. ..	810 – 811	195. Oct. 4, 810.
733	3912	Khara	.. ..	811 – 812	196. Sept. 23, 811.
734	3913	Nandana ..	.. ..	812 – 813	197. Sept. 12, 812.
735	3914	Vijaya	.. ..	813 – 814	198. Sept. 1, 813.
736	3915	Jaya	.. ..	814 – 815	199. Aug. 22, 814.
737	3916	Manmadha ..	.. ..	815 – 816	200. Aug. 11, 815.
738	3917	Durmukhi ..	.. ..	816 – 817	201. July 30, 816.
739	3918	Hevilaṁbi ..	.. ..	817 – 818	202. July 20, 817.
740	3919	Vilaṁbi	.. ..	818 – 819	203. July 9, 818.
741	3920	Vikāri	.. ..	819 – 820	204. June 28, 819.
742	3921	Śārvari	.. ..	820 – 821	205. June 17, 820.
743	3922	Plava	.. ..	821 – 822	206. June 6, 821.
744	3923	Śubhakṛit ..	.. ..	822 – 823	207. May 27, 822.
745	3924	Śobhana, or -kṛit.	.. ..	823 – 824	208. May 16, 823.
746	3925	Krodhi	1	824 – 825	209. May 4, 824.
747	3926	Viśvāvasu ..	1 — 2	825 – 826	210. April 24, 825.
748	3927	Parābhava ..	2 — 3	826 – 827	211. April 13, 826.
749	3928	Plavaṅga ..	3 — 4	827 – 828	212. April 2, 827.
750	3929	Kīlaka	4 — 5	828 – 829	213. March 22, 828.
751	3930	Saumya ..	5 — 6	829 – 830	214. March 11, 829.
752	3931	Sādhāraṇa ..	6 — 7	830 – 831	215. Feb. 28, 830.
753	3932	Virodhikṛit ..	7 — 8	831 – 832	216. Feb. 18, 831.
754	3933	Parīdhāvi, or -pi.	8 — 9	832 – 833	217. Feb. 7, 832.
755	9934	Pramādīcha ..	9 — 10	833 – 834	218. Jan. 27, 833.
756	3935	Ānanda ..	10 — 11	834 – 835	219. Jan. 16, 834.
757	3936	Rākshasa ..	11 — 12	835 – 836	220. Jan. 5, 835.
758	3937	Nala	12 — 13	836 – 837	221. Dec. 26, 835. 222. Dec. 14, 836.
759	3938	Piṅgala	13 — 14	837 – 838	223. Dec. 3, 837.
760	3939	Kālayukti ..	14 — 15	838 – 839	224. Nov. 23, 838.
761	3940	Siddhārthi ..	15 — 16	839 – 840	225. Nov. 12, 839.
762	3941	Raudri	16 — 17	840 – 841	226. Oct. 31, 840.
763	3942	Durmati ..	17 — 18	841 – 842	227. Oct. 21, 841.
764	3943	Dundubhi ..	18 — 19	842 – 843	228. Oct. 10, 842.
765	3944	Rudhirodgāri ..	19 — 20	843 – 844	229. Sept. 30, 843.

Year of the *Śālivāhana Śaka.*	Year of the *Kaliyuga.*	Cyclic Year.	*Kollam Āṇḍu*, or Era of Quilon.	Christian Era (A.D.)	The *Hijra* Year commences.
766	3945	Raktākshi ..	20 — 21	844 — 845	230. Sept. 18, 844.
767	3946	Krodhana ..	21 — 22	845 — 846	231. Sept. 7, 845.
768	3947	Akshaya	22 — 23	846 — 847	232. Aug. 28, 846.
769	3948	Prabhava ..	23 — 24	847 — 848	233. Aug. 17, 847.
770	3949	Vibhava	24 — 25	848 — 849	234. Aug. 5, 848.
771	3950	Śukla	25 — 26	849 — 850	235. July 26, 849.
772	3951	Pramodūta ..	26 — 27	850 — 851	236. July 15, 850.
773	3952	Prajotpatti ..	27 — 28	851 — 852	237. July 5, 851.
774	3953	Āngirasa ..	28 — 29	852 — 853	238. June 23, 852.
775	3954	Śrīmukha ..	29 — 30	853 — 854	239. June 12, 853.
776	3955	Bhava	30 — 31	854 — 855	240. June 2, 854.
777	3956	Yuva	31 — 32	855 — 856	241. May 22, 855.
778	3957	Dhātu	32 — 33	856 — 857	242. May 10, 856.
779	3958	Īśvara	33 — 34	857 — 858	243. April 30, 857.
780	3959	Bahudhānya ..	34 — 35	858 — 859	244. April 19, 858.
781	3960	Pramādhi ..	35 — 36	859 — 860	245. April 8, 859.
782	3961	Vikrama	36 — 37	860 — 861	246. March 28, 860.
783	3962	Vishu, or Vṛishu.	37 — 38	861 — 862	247. March 17, 861.
784	3963	Chitrabhānu ..	38 — 39	862 — 863	248. March 7, 862.
785	3964	Subhānu	39 — 40	863 — 864	249. Feb. 24, 863.
786	3965	Tāraṇa	40 — 41	864 — 865	250. Feb. 13, 864.
787	3966	Pārthiva	41 — 42	865 — 866	251. Feb. 2, 865.
788	3967	Vyaya	42 — 43	866 — 867	252. Jan. 22, 866.
789	3968	Sarvajit	43 — 44	867 — 868	253. Jan. 11, 867.
790	3969	Sarvadhāri ..	44 — 45	868 — 869	254. Jan. 1, 868.
791	3970	Virodhi	45 — 46	869 — 870	255. Dec. 20, 868. 256. Dec. 10, 869.
792	3971	Vikṛiti	46 — 47	870 — 871	257. Nov. 29, 870.
793	3972	Khara	47 — 48	871 — 872	258. Nov. 18, 871.
794	3973	Nandana ..	48 — 49	872 — 873	259. Nov. 7, 872.
795	3974	Vijaya	49 — 50	873 — 874	260. Oct. 27, 873.
796	3975	Jaya	50 — 51	874 — 875	261. Oct. 16, 874.
797	3976	Manmadha ..	51 — 52	875 — 876	262. Oct. 6, 875.
798	3977	Durmukhi ..	52 — 53	876 — 877	263. Sept. 24, 876.
799	3978	Hevilambi ..	53 — 54	877 — 878	264. Sept. 13, 1877.
800	3979	Vilambi	54 — 55	878 — 879	265. Sept. 3, 878.
801	3980	Vikāri	55 — 56	879 — 880	266. Aug. 23, 879.
802	3981	Śārvari	56 — 57	880 — 881	267. Aug. 12, 880.
803	3982	Plava	57 — 58	881 — 882	268. Aug. 1, 881.

Year of the *Śālivāhana Śaka.*	Year of the *Kaliyuga.*	Cyclic Year.	*Kollam Āṇḍu*, or Era of Quilon.	Christian Era (A.D.)	The *Hijra* Year commences.
804	3983	Śubhakṛit ..	58 — 59	882 – 883	269. July 21, 882.
805	3984	Śobhana, or -kṛit.	59 — 60	883 – 884	270. July 11, 883.
806	3985	Krodhi	60 — 61	884 – 885	271. June 29, 884.
807	3986	Viśvāvasu ..	61 — 62	885 – 886	272. June 18, 885.
808	3987	Parābhava ..	62 — 63	886 – 887	273. June 8, 886.
809	3988	Plavaṅga ..	63 — 64	887 – 888	274. May 28, 887.
810	3989	Kīlaka	64 — 65	888 – 889	275. May 16, 888.
811	3990	Saumya	65 — 66	889 – 890	276. May 6, 889.
812	3991	Sādhāraṇa ..	66 — 67	890 – 891	277. April 25, 890.
813	3992	Virodhikṛit ..	67 — 68	891 – 892	278. April 15, 891.
814	3993	Parīdhāvi, or -pi.	68 — 69	892 – 893	279. April 3, 892.
815	3994	Pramādīcha ..	69 — 70	893 – 894	280. March 23, 893.
816	3995	Ānanda	70 — 71	894 – 895	281. March 13, 894.
817	3996	Rākshasa ..	71 — 72	895 – 896	282. March 2, 895.
818	3997	Nala	72 — 73	896 – 897	283. Feb. 19, 896.
819	3998	Piṅgala	73 — 74	897 – 898	284. Feb. 8, 897.
820	3999	Kālayukti ..	74 — 75	898 – 899	285. Jan. 28, 898.
821	4000	Siddhārthi ..	75 — 76	899 – 900	286. Jan. 17, 899.
822	4001	Raudri	76 — 77	900 – 901	287. Jan. 7, 900.
823	4002	Durmati ..	77 — 78	901 – 902	288. Dec. 26, 900. 289. Dec. 16, 901.
824	4003	Dundubhi ..	78 — 79	902 – 903	290. Dec. 5, 902.
825	4004	Rudhirodgāri ..	79 — 80	903 – 904	291. Nov. 24, 903.
826	4005	Raktākshi ..	80 — 81	904 – 905	292. Nov. 13, 904.
827	4006	Krodhana ..	81 — 82	905 – 906	293. Nov. 2, 905.
828	4007	Akshaya	82 — 83	906 – 907	294. Oct. 22, 906.
829	4008	Prabhava ..	83 — 84	907 – 908	295. Oct. 12, 907.
830	4009	Vibhava	84 — 85	908 – 909	296. Sept. 30, 908.
831	4010	Śukla	85 — 86	909 – 910	297. Sept. 20, 909.
832	4011	Pramodūta ..	86 — 87	910 – 911	298. Sept. 9, 910.
833	4012	Prajotpatti ..	87 — 88	911 – 912	299. Aug. 29, 911.
834	4013	Āṅgirasa ..	88 — 89	912 – 913	300. Aug. 18, 912.
835	4014	Śrīmukha ..	89 — 90	913 – 914	301. Aug. 7, 913.
836	4015	Bhava	90 — 91	914 – 915	302. July 27, 914.
837	4016	Yuva	91 — 92	915 – 916	303. July 17, 915.
838	4017	Dhātu	92 — 93	916 – 917	304. July 5, 916.
839	4018	Īśvara	93 — 94	917 – 918	305. June 24, 917.
840	4019	Bahudhānya ..	94 — 95	918 – 919	306. June 14, 918.
841	4020	Pramādhi ..	95 — 96	919 – 920	307. June 3, 919.

Year of the *Śālivāhana Śaka.*	Year of the *Kaliyuga.*	Cyclic Year.	*Kollam Āṇḍu*; or Era of Quilon.	Christian Era (A.D.)	The *Hijra* Year commences.
842	4021	Vikrama	96 — 97	920 – 921	308. May 23, 920.
843	4022	Vishu, or Vṛishu.	97 — 98	921 – 922	309. May 12, 921.
844	4023	Chitrabhānu ..	98 — 99	922 – 923	310. May 1, 922.
845	4024	Subhānu	99 — 100	923 – 924	311. April 21, 923.
846	4025	Tāraṇa	100 — 101	924 – 965	312. April 9, 924.
847	4026	Pārthiva	101 — 102	925 – 926	313. March 29, 925.
848	4027	Vyaya	102 — 103	926 – 927	314. March 19, 926.
849	4028	Sarvajit	103 — 104	927 – 928	315. March 8, 927.
850	4029	Sarvadhāri ..	104 — 105	928 – 929	316. Feb. 25, 928.
851	4030	Virodhi	105 — 106	929 – 930	317. Feb. 14, 929.
852	4031	Vikṛiti	106 — 107	930 – 931	318. Feb. 3, 930.
853	4032	Khara	107 — 108	931 – 932	319. Jan. 24, 931.
854	4033	Nandana ..	108 — 109	932 – 933	320. Jan. 13, 932.
855	4034	Vijaya	109 — 110	933 – 934	321. Jan. 2, 933.
856	4035	Jaya	110 — 111	934 – 935	322. Dec. 22, 933. 323. Dec. 11, 934.
857	4036	Manmadha ..	111 — 112	935 – 936	324. Nov. 30, 935.
858	4037	Durmukhi ..	112 — 113	936 – 937	325. Nov. 19, 936.
859	4038	Hevilambi ..	113 — 114	937 – 938	326. Nov. 8, 937.
860	4039	Vilambi	114 — 115	938 – 939	327. Oct. 29, 938.
861	4040	Vikāri	115 — 116	939 – 940	328. Oct. 18, 939.
862	4041	Śārvari	116 — 117	940 – 941	329. Oct. 6, 940.
863	4042	Plava	117 — 118	941 – 942	330. Sept. 26, 941.
864	4043	Śubhakṛit ..	118 — 119	942 – 943	331. Sept. 15, 942.
865	4044	Śōbhana, or -kṛit.	119 — 120	943 – 944	362. Sept. 4, 943.
866	4045	Krodhi	120 — 121	944 – 945	333. Aug. 24, 944.
867	4046	Viśvāvasu ..	121 — 122	945 – 946	334. Aug. 13, 945.
868	4047	Parābhava ..	122 — 123	946 – 947	335. Aug. 2, 946.
869	4048	Plavaṅga ..	123 — 124	947 – 948	336. July 23, 947.
870	4049	Kīlaka	124 — 125	948 – 949	337. July 11, 948.
871	4050	Saumya	125 — 126	949 – 950	338. July 5, 949.
872	4051	Sādhāraṇa ..	126 — 127	950 – 951	339. June 20, 950.
873	4052	Virodhikṛit ..	127 — 128	951 – 952	340. June 9, 951.
874	4053	Parīdhāvi, or -pi.	128 — 129	952 – 953	341. May 29, 952.
875	4054	Pramādīcha ..	129 — 130	953 – 954	342. May 18, 953.
876	4055	Ānanda	130 — 131	954 – 955	343. May 7, 954.
877	4056	Rākshasa ..	131 — 132	955 – 956	344. April 27, 955.
878	4057	Nala	132 — 133	956 – 957	345. April 15, 956.
879	4058	Piṅgala	133 — 134	957 – 958	346. April 4, 957.

Year of the *Sálivāhana Śaka*.	Year of the *Kaliyuga*.	Cyclic Year.	*Kollam Āndu*, or Era of Quilon.	Christian Era (A.D.)	The *Hijra* Year commences.
880	4059	Kālayukti ..	134 — 135	958 – 959	347. March 25, 958.
881	4060	Siddhārthi ..	135 — 136	959 – 960	348. March 14, 959.
882	4061	Raudri	136 — 137	960 – 961	349. March 3, 960.
883	4062	Durmati	137 — 138	961 – 962	350. Feb. 20, 961.
884	4063	Dundubhi ..	138 — 139	962 – 963	351. Feb. 9, 962.
885	4064	Rudhirodgāri ..	139 — 140	963 – 964	352. Jan. 30, 963.
886	4065	Raktākshi ..	140 — 141	964 – 965	353. Jan. 19, 964.
887	4066	Krodhana ..	141 — 142	965 – 966	354. Jan. 7, 965.
888	4067	Akshaya	142 — 143	966 – 967	355. Dec. 28, 965. 356. Dec. 17, 966.
889	4068	Prabhava ..	143 — 144	967 – 968	357. Dec. 7, 967.
890	4069	Vibhava	144 — 145	968 – 969	358. Nov. 25, 968.
891	4070	Śukla	145 — 146	969 – 970	359. Nov. 14, 969.
892	4071	Pramodūta ..	146 — 147	970 – 971	360. Nov. 4, 970.
893	4072	Prajotpatti ..	147 — 148	971 – 972	361. Oct. 24, 971.
894	4073	Āṅgirasa ..	148 — 149	972 – 973	362. Oct. 12, 972.
895	4074	Śrīmukha ..	149 — 150	973 – 974	363. Oct. 2, 973.
896	4075	Bhava	150 — 151	974 – 975	364. Sept. 21, 974.
897	4076	Yuva	151 — 152	975 – 976	365. Sept. 10, 975.
898	4077	Dhātu	152 — 153	976 – 977	366. Aug. 30, 976.
899	4078	Īśvara	153 — 154	977 – 978	367. Aug. 19, 977.
900	4079	Bahudhānya ..	154 — 155	978 – 979	368. Aug. 9, 978.
901	4080	Pramādhi ..	155 — 156	979 – 980	369. July 29, 979.
902	4081	Vikrama	156 — 157	980 – 981	370. July 17, 980.
903	4082	Vishu, or Vṛishu.	157 — 158	981 – 982	371. July 7, 981.
904	4083	Chitrabhānu ..	158 — 159	982 – 983	372. June 26, 982.
905	4084	Subhānu	159 — 160	983 – 984	373. June 15, 983.
906	4085	Tāraṇa	160 — 161	984 – 985	374. June 4, 984.
907	4086	Pārthiva	161 — 162	985 – 986	375. May 24, 985.
908	4087	Vyaya	162 — 163	986 – 987	376. May 13, 986.
909	4088	Sarvajit	163 — 164	987 – 988	377. May 3, 987.
910	4089	Sarvadhāri ..	164 — 165	988 – 989	378. April 21, 988.
911	4090	Virodhi	165 — 166	989 – 990	379. April 11, 989.
912	4091	Vikṛiti	166 — 167	990 – 991	380. March 31, 990.
913	4092	Khara	167 — 168	991 – 992	381. March 20, 991.
914	4093	Nandana ..	168 — 169	992 – 993	382. March 9, 992.
915	4094	Vijaya	169 — 170	993 – 994	383. Feb. 26, 993.
916	4095	Jaya	170 — 171	994 – 995	384. Feb. 15, 994.
917	4096	Manmadha ..	171 — 172	995 – 996	385. Feb. 5, 995.

Year of the *Śālivāhana Śaka.*	Year of the *Kaliyuga.*	Cyclic Year.	*Kollam Āṇḍu*, or Era of Quilon.	Christian Era (A.D.)	The *Hijra* Year commences.
918	4097	Durmukhi ..	172 — 173	996 — 997	386. Jan. 25, 996.
919	4098	Hevilambi ..	173 — 174	997 — 998	387. Jan. 14, 997.
920	4099	Vilambi	174 — 175	998 — 999	388. Jan. 3, 998.
921	4100	Vikāri	175 — 176	999 — 1000	389. Dec. 23, 998. 390. Dec. 13, 999.
922	4101	Śārvari	176 — 177	1000 — 1001	391. Dec. 1, 1000.
923	4102	Plava	177 — 178	1001 — 1002	392. Nov. 20, 1001.
924	4103	Śubhakṛit ..	178 — 179	1002 — 1003	393. Nov. 10, 1002.
925	4104	Śobhana, or -kṛit.	179 — 180	1003 — 1004	394. Oct. 30, 1003.
926	4105	Krodhi	180 — 181	1004 — 1005	395. Oct. 18, 1004.
927	4106	Viśvāvasu ..	181 — 182	1005 — 1006	396. Oct. 8, 1005.
928	4107	Parābhava ..	182 — 183	1006 — 1007	397. Sept. 27, 1006.
929	4108	Plavaṅga ..	183 — 184	1007 — 1008	398. Sept. 17, 1007.
930	4109	Kīlaka	184 — 185	1008 — 1009	399. Sept. 5, 1008.
931	4110	Saumya	185 — 186	1009 — 1010	400. Aug. 25, 1009.
932	4111	Sādhāraṇa ..	186 — 187	1010 — 1011	401. Aug. 15, 1010.
933	4112	Virodhikṛit ..	187 — 188	1011 — 1012	402. Aug. 4, 1011.
934	4113	Parīdhāvi, or -pi..	188 — 189	1012 — 1013	403. July 23, 1012.
935	4114	Pramādīcha ..	189 — 190	1013 — 1014	404. July 13, 1013.
936	4115	Ānanda	190 — 191	1014 — 1015	405. July 2, 1014.
937	4116	Rākshasa ..	191 — 192	1015 — 1016	406. June 21, 1015.
938	4117	Nala	192 — 193	1016 — 1017	407. June 10, 1016.
939	4118	Piṅgala	193 — 194	1017 — 1018	408. May 30, 1017.
940	4119	Kālayukti ..	194 — 195	1018 — 1019	409. May 20, 1018.
941	4120	Siddhārthi ..	195 — 196	1019 — 1020	410. May 9, 1019.
942	4121	Raudri	196 — 197	1020 — 1021	411. April 27, 1020.
943	4122	Durmati	197 — 198	1021 — 1022	412. April 17, 1021.
944	4123	Dundubhi ..	198 — 199	1022 — 1023	413. April 6, 1022.
945	4124	Rudhirodgāri ..	199 — 200	1023 — 1024	414. March 26, 1023.
946	4125	Raktākshi ..	200 — 201	1024 — 1025	415. March 15, 1024.
947	4126	Krodhana ..	201 — 202	1025 — 1026	416. March 4, 1025.
948	4127	Akshaya	202 — 203	1026 — 1027	417. Feb. 22, 1026.
949	4128	Prabhava ..	203 — 204	1027 — 1028	418. Feb. 11, 1027.
950	4129	Vibhava	204 — 205	1028 — 1029	419. Jan. 31, 1028.
951	4130	Śukla	205 — 206	1029 — 1030	420. Jan. 20, 1029.
952	4131	Pramodūta ..	206 — 207	1030 — 1031	421. Jan. 9, 1030.
953	4132	Prajotpatti ..	207 — 208	1031 — 1032	422. Dec. 29, 1030. 423. Dec. 19, 1031.
954	4133	Āṅgirasa ..	208 — 209	1032 — 1033	424. Dec. 7, 1032.

Year of the Śâlivâhana Śaka.	Year of the Kaliyuga.	Cyclic Year.	Kollam Ându, or Era of Quilon.	Christian Era (A.D.)	The Hijra Year commences.
955	4134	Śrîmukha ..	209 — 210	1033 – 1034	425. Nov. 26, 1033.
956	4135	Bhava	210 — 211	1034 – 1035	426. Nov. 16, 1034.
957	4136	Yuva	211 — 212	1035 – 1036	427. Nov. 5, 1035.
958	4137	Dhâtu	212 — 213	1036 – 1037	428. Oct. 25, 1036.
959	4138	Îśvara	213 — 214	1037 – 1038	429. Oct. 14, 1037.
960	4139	Bahudhânya ..	214 — 215	1038 – 1039	430. Oct. 3, 1038.
961	4140	Pramâdhi ..	215 — 216	1039 – 1040	431. Sept. 23, 1039.
962	4141	Vikrama	216 — 217	1040 – 1041	432. Sept. 11, 1040.
963	4142	Vishu, or Vṛishu ..	217 — 218	1041 – 1042	433. Aug. 31, 1041.
964	4143	Chitrabhânu ..	218 — 219	1042 – 1043	434. Aug. 21, 1042.
965	4144	Subhânu ..	219 — 220	1043 – 1044	435. Aug. 10, 1043.
966	4145	Târaṇa	220 — 221	1044 – 1045	436. July 29, 1044.
967	4146	Pârthiva	221 — 222	1045 – 1046	437. July 19, 1045.
968	4147	Vyaya	222 — 223	1046 – 1047	438. July 8, 1046.
969	4148	Sarvajit	223 — 224	1047 – 1048	439. June 28, 1047.
970	4149	Sarvadhâri ..	224 — 225	1048 – 1049	440. June 16, 1048.
971	4150	Virodhi	225 — 226	1049 – 1050	441. June 5, 1049.
972	4151	Vikṛiti	226 — 227	1050 – 1051	442. May 26, 1050.
973	4152	Khara	227 — 228	1051 – 1052	443. May 15, 1051.
974	4153	Nandana ..	228 — 229	1052 – 1053	444. May 3, 1052.
975	4154	Vijaya	229 — 230	1053 – 1054	445. April 23, 1053.
976	4155	Jaya	230 — 231	1054 – 1055	446. April 12, 1054.
977	4156	Manmadha ..	231 — 232	1055 – 1056	447. April 2, 1055.
978	4157	Durmukhi ..	232 — 233	1056 – 1057	448. March 21, 1056.
979	4158	Hevilambi ..	233 — 234	1057 – 1058	449. March 10, 1057.
980	4159	Vilambi	234 — 235	1058 – 1059	450. Feb. 28, 1058.
981	4160	Vikâri	235 — 236	1059 – 1060	451. Feb. 17, 1059.
982	4161	Śârvari	236 — 237	1060 – 1061	452. Feb. 6, 1060.
983	4162	Plava	237 — 238	1061 – 1062	453. Jan. 26, 1061.
984	4163	Śubhakṛit ..	238 — 239	1062 – 1063	454. Jan. 15, 1062.
985	4164	Śobhana, or -kṛit.	239 — 240	1063 – 1064	455. Jan. 4, 1063.
986	4165	Krodhi	240 — 241	1064 – 1065	456. Dec. 25, 1063. 457. Dec. 13, 1064.
987	4166	Viśvâvasu ..	241 — 242	1065 – 1066	458. Dec. 3, 1065.
988	4167	Parâbhava ..	242 — 243	1066 – 1067	459. Nov. 22, 1066.
989	4168	Plavaṅga ..	243 — 244	1067 – 1068	460. Nov. 11, 1067.
990	4169	Kîlaka	244 — 245	1068 – 1069	461. Oct. 31, 1068.
991	4170	Saumya	245 — 246	1069 – 1070	462. Oct. 20, 1069.
992	4171	Sâdhâraṇa ..	246 — 247	1070 – 1071	463. Oct. 9, 1070.

Year of the *Śālivāhana Śaka.*	Year of the *Kaliyuga.*	Cyclic Year.	*Kollam Āṇḍu*, or Era of Quilon.	Christian Era (A.D.)	The *Hijra* Year commences.
993	4172	Virodhikṛit ..	247 — 248	1071 – 1072	464. Sept. 29, 1071.
994	4173	Parīdhāvi, or -pi.	248 — 249	1072 – 1073	465. Sept. 17, 1072.
995	4174	Pramādīcha ..	249 — 250	1073 – 1074	466. Sept. 6, 1073.
996	4175	Ānanda	250 — 251	1074 – 1075	467. Aug. 27, 1074.
997	4176	Rākshasa ..	251 — 252	1075 – 1076	468. Aug. 16, 1075.
998	4177	Nala	252 — 253	1076 – 1077	469. Aug. 5, 1076.
999	4178	Piṅgala	253 — 254	1077 – 1078	470. July 25, 1077.
1000	4179	Kālayukti ..	254 — 255	1078 – 1079	471. July 14, 1078.
1001	4180	Siddhārthi ..	255 — 256	1079 – 1080	472. July 4, 1079.
1002	4181	Raudri	256 — 257	1080 – 1081	473. June 22, 1080.
1003	4182	Durmati	257 — 258	1081 – 1082	474. June 11, 1081.
1004	4183	Dundubhi ..	258 — 259	1082 – 1083	475. June 1, 1082.
1005	4184	Rudhirodgāri ..	259 — 260	1083 – 1084	476. May 21, 1083.
1006	4185	Raktākshi ..	260 — 261	1084 - 1085	477. May 10, 1084.
1007	4186	Krodhana ..	261 — 262	1085 – 1086	478. April 29, 1085.
1008	4187	Akshaya	262 — 263	1086 – 1087	479. April 18, 1086.
1009	4188	Prabhava ..	263 — 264	1087 – 1088	480. April 8, 1087.
1010	4189	Vibhava	264 — 265	1088 – 1089	481. March 27, 1088.
1011	4190	Śukla	265 — 266	1089 – 1090	482. March 16, 1089.
1012	4191	Pramodūta ..	266 — 267	1090 – 1091	483. March 6, 1090.
1013	4192	Prajotpatti ..	267 — 268	1091 – 1092	484. Feb. 23, 1091.
1014	4193	Āṅgirasa ..	268 — 269	1092 – 1093	485. Feb. 12, 1092.
1015	4194	Śrīmukha ..	269 — 270	1093 – 1094	486. Feb. 1, 1093.
1016	4195	Bhava	270 — 271	1094 – 1095	487. Jan. 21, 1094.
1017	4196	Yuva	271 — 272	1095 – 1096	488. Jan. 11, 1095.
1018	4197	Dhātu	272 — 273	1096 – 1097	{ 489. Dec. 31, 1095. 490. Dec. 19, 1096.
1019	4198	Īśvara	273 — 274	1097 – 1098	491. Dec. 9, 1097.
1020	4199	Bahudhānya ..	274 — 275	1098 – 1099	492. Nov. 28, 1098.
1021	4200	Pramādhi ..	275 — 276	1099 – 1100	493. Nov. 17, 1099.
1022	4201	Vikrama	276 — 277	1100 – 1101	494. Nov. 6, 1100.
1023	4202	Vishu, or Vṛishu ..	277 — 278	1101 – 1102	495. Oct. 26, 1101.
1024	4203	Chitrabhānu ..	278 — 279	1102 – 1103	496. Oct. 15, 1102.
1025	4204	Subhānu ..	279 — 280	1103 – 1104	497. Oct. 5, 1103.
1026	4205	Tāraṇa	280 — 281	1104 – 1105	498. Sept. 23, 1104.
1027	4206	Pārthiva	281 — 282	1105 – 1106	499. Sept. 13, 1105.
1028	4207	Vyaya	282 — 283	1106 – 1107	500. Sept. 2, 1106.
1029	4208	Sarvajit	283 — 284	1107 – 1108	501. Aug. 22, 1107.
1030	4209	Sarvadhāri ..	284 — 285	1108 – 1109	502. Aug. 11, 1108.

Year of the *Śālivāhana Śaka.*	Year of the *Kaliyuga.*	Cyclic Year.	*Kollaṁ Āṇḍu*, or Era of Quilon.	Christian Era (A.D.)	The *Hijra* Year commences.
1031	4210	Virodhi	285 — 286	1109 — 1110	503. Aug. 1, 1109.
1032	4211	Vikṛiti	286 — 287	1110 — 1111	504. July 20, 1110.
1033	4212	Khara	287 — 288	1111 — 1112	505. July 10, 1111.
1034	4213	Nandana ..	288 — 289	1112 — 1113	506. June 28, 1112.
1035	4214	Vijaya	289 — 290	1113 — 1114	507. June 18, 1113.
1036	4215	Jaya	290 — 291	1114 — 1115	508. June 7, 1114.
1037	4216	Manmadha ..	291 — 292	1115 — 1116	509. May 27, 1115.
1038	4217	Durmukhi ..	292 — 293	1116 — 1117	510. May 16, 1116.
1039	4218	Hevilaṁbi ..	293 — 294	1117 — 1118	511. May 5, 1117.
1040	4219	Vilaṁbi	294 — 295	1118 — 1119	512. April 24, 1118.
1041	4220	Vikāri	295 — 296	1119 — 1120	513. April 14, 1119.
1042	4221	Śārvari	296 — 297	1120 — 1121	514. April 2, 1120.
1043	4222	Plava	297 — 298	1121 — 1122	515. March 22, 1121.
1044	4223	Śubhakṛit ..	298 — 299	1122 — 1123	516. March 12, 1122.
1045	4224	Śobhana, or -kṛit.	299 — 300	1123 — 1124	517. March 1, 1123.
1046	4225	Krodhi	300 — 301	1124 — 1125	518. Feb. 19, 1124.
1047	4226	Viśvāvasu ..	301 — 302	1125 — 1126	519. Feb. 7, 1125.
1048	4227	Parābhava ..	302 — 303	1126 — 1127	520. Jan. 27, 1126.
1049	4228	Plavaṅga ..	303 — 304	1127 — 1128	521. Jan. 17, 1127.
1050	4229	Kīlaka	304 — 305	1128 — 1129	522. Jan. 6, 1128.
1051	4230	Saumya	305 — 306	1129 — 1130	523. Dec. 25, 1128. 524. Dec. 15, 1129.
1052	4231	Sādhāraṇa ..	306 — 307	1130 — 1131	525. Dec. 4, 1130.
1053	4232	Virodhikṛit ..	307 — 308	1131 — 1132	526. Nov. 23, 1131.
1054	4233	Parīdhāvi, or -pi.	308 — 309	1132 — 1133	527. Nov. 12, 1132.
1055	4234	Pramādīcha ..	309 — 310	1133 — 1134	528. Nov. 1, 1133.
1056	4235	Ānanda	310 — 311	1134 — 1135	529. Oct. 22, 1134.
1057	4236	Rākshasa ..	311 — 312	1135 — 1136	530. Oct. 10, 1135.
1058	4237	Nala	312 — 313	1136 — 1137	531. Sept. 29, 1136.
1059	4238	Piṅgala	313 — 314	1137 — 1138	532. Sept. 19, 1137.
1060	4239	Kālayukti ..	314 — 315	1138 — 1139	533. Sept. 8, 1138.
1061	4240	Siddhārthi ..	315 — 316	1139 — 1140	534. Aug. 28, 1139.
1062	4241	Raudri	316 — 317	1140 — 1141	535. Aug. 17, 1140.
1063	4242	Durmati	317 — 318	1141 — 1142	536. Aug. 6, 1141.
1064	4243	Dundubhi ..	318 — 319	1142 — 1143	537. July 27, 1142.
1065	4244	Rudhirodgāri ..	319 — 320	1143 — 1144	538. July 16, 1143.
1066	4245	Raktākshi ..	320 — 321	1144 — 1145	539. July 4, 1144.
1067	4246	Krodhana ..	321 — 322	1145 — 1146	540. June 24, 1145.
1068	4247	Akshaya	322 — 323	1146 — 1147	541. June 13, 1146.

Year of the *Śālivāhana Śaka*.	Year of the *Kaliyuga*.	Cyclic Year.	*Kollam Āndu*, or Era of Quilon.	Christian Era (A.D.)	The *Hijra* Year commences.
1069	4248	Prabhava ..	323 — 324	1147 — 1148	542. June 2, 1147.
1070	4249	Vibhava	324 — 325	1148 — 1149	543. May 22, 1148.
1071	4250	Śukla	325 — 326	1149 — 1150	544. May 11, 1149.
1072	4251	Pramodūta ..	326 — 327	1150 — 1151	545. April 30, 1150.
1073	4252	Prajotpatti ..	327 — 328	1151 — 1152	546. April 20, 1151.
1074	4253	Āṅgirasa	328 — 329	1152 — 1153	547. April 8, 1152.
1075	4254	Śrīmukha ..	329 — 330	1153 — 1154	548. March 29, 1153.
1076	4255	Bhava	330 — 331	1154 — 1155	549. March 18, 1154.
1077	4256	Yuva	331 — 332	1155 — 1156	550. March 7, 1155.
1078	4257	Dhātu	332 — 333	1156 — 1157	551. Feb. 25, 1156.
1079	4258	Īśvara	333 — 334	1157 — 1158	552. Feb. 13, 1157.
1080	4259	Bahudhānya ..	334 — 335	1158 — 1159	553. Feb. 2, 1158.
1081	4260	Pramādhi ..	335 — 336	1159 — 1160	554. Jan. 23, 1159.
1082	4261	Vikrama	336 — 337	1160 — 1161	555. Jan. 12, 1160.
1083	4262	Vishu, or Vṛishu.	337 — 338	1161 — 1162	556. Dec. 31, 1160. 557. Dec. 21, 1161.
1084	4263	Chitrabhānu ..	338 — 339	1162 — 1163	558. Dec. 10, 1162.
1085	4264	Subhānu ..	339 — 340	1163 — 1164	559. Nov. 30, 1163.
1086	4265	Tāraṇa	340 — 341	1164 — 1165	560. Nov. 18, 1164.
1087	4266	Pārthiva	341 — 342	1165 — 1166	561. Nov. 7, 1165.
1088	4267	Vyaya	342 — 343	1166 — 1167	562. Oct. 28, 1166.
1089	4268	Sarvajit	343 — 344	1167 — 1168	563. Oct. 17, 1167.
1090	4269	Sarvadhāri ..	344 — 345	1168 — 1169	564. Oct. 5, 1168.
1091	4270	Virodhi	345 — 346	1169 — 1170	565. Sept. 25, 1169.
1092	4271	Vikṛiti	346 — 347	1170 — 1171	566. Sept. 14, 1170.
1093	4272	Khara	347 — 348	1171 — 1172	567. Sept. 4, 1171.
1094	4273	Nandana ..	348 — 349	1172 — 1173	568. Aug. 23, 1172.
1095	4274	Vijaya	349 — 350	1173 — 1174	569. Aug. 12, 1173.
1096	4275	Jaya	350 — 351	1174 — 1175	570. Aug. 2, 1174.
1097	4276	Manmadha ..	351 — 352	1175 — 1176	571. July 22, 1175.
1098	4277	Durmukhi ..	352 — 353	1176 — 1177	572. July 10, 1176.
1099	4278	Hevilaṁbi ..	353 — 354	1177 — 1178	573. June 30, 1177.
1100	4279	Vilaṁbi	354 — 355	1178 — 1179	574. June 19, 1178.
1101	4280	Vikāri	355 — 356	1179 — 1180	575. June 8, 1179.
1102	4281	Śārvari	356 — 357	1180 — 1181	576. May 28, 1180.
1103	4282	Plava	357 — 358	1181 — 1182	577. May 17, 1181.
1104	4283	Śubhakṛit ..	358 — 359	1182 — 1183	578. May 7, 1182.
1105	4284	Śobhana, or -kṛit.	359 — 360	1183 — 1184	579. April 26, 1183.
1106	4285	Krodhi	360 — 361	1184 — 1185	580. April 14, 1184.

Year of the *Śālivāhana Śaka*.	Year of the *Kaliyuga*.	Cyclic Year.	*Kollam Āṇḍu*, or Era of Quilon.	Christian Era (A.D.)	The *Hijra* Year commences.
1107	4286	Viśvāvasu ..	361 — 362	1185 – 1186	581. April 4, 1185.
1108	4287	Parābhava ..	362 — 363	1186 – 1187	582. March 24, 1186.
1109	4288	Plavaṅga ..	363 — 364	1187 – 1188	583. March 13, 1187.
1110	4289	Kīlaka	364 — 365	1188 – 1189	584. March 2, 1188.
1111	4290	Saumya	365 — 366	1189 – 1190	585. Feb. 19, 1189.
1112	4291	Sādhāraṇa ..	366 — 367	1190 – 1191	586. Feb. 8, 1190.
1113	4292	Virodhikṛit ..	367 — 368	1191 – 1192	587. Jan. 29, 1191.
1114	4293	Parīdhāvi, or -pi.	368 — 369	1192 – 1193	588. Jan. 18, 1192.
1115	4294	Pramādīcha ..	369 — 370	1193 – 1194	589. Jan. 7, 1193.
1116	4295	Ānanda	370 — 371	1194 – 1195	590. Dec. 27, 1193. 591. Dec. 16, 1194.
1117	4296	Rākshasa ..	371 — 372	1195 – 1196	592. Dec. 6, 1195.
1118	4297	Nala	372 — 373	1196 – 1197	593. Nov. 24, 1196.
1119	4298	Piṅgala	373 — 374	1197 – 1198	594. Nov. 13, 1197.
1120	4299	Kālayukti ..	374 — 375	1198 – 1199	595. Nov. 3, 1198.
1121	4300	Siddhārthi ..	375 — 376	1199 – 1200	596. Oct. 23, 1199.
1122	4301	Raudri	376 — 377	1200 – 1201	597. Oct. 12, 1200.
1123	4302	Durmati	377 — 378	1201 – 1202	598. Oct. 1, 1201.
1124	4303	Dundubhi ..	378 — 379	1202 – 1203	599. Sept. 20, 1202.
1125	4304	Rudhirodgāri ..	379 — 380	1203 – 1204	600. Sept. 10, 1203.
1126	4305	Raktākshi ..	380 — 381	1204 – 1205	601. Aug. 29, 1204.
1127	4306	Krodhana ..	381 — 382	1205 – 1206	602. Aug. 18, 1205.
1128	4307	Akshaya	382 — 383	1206 – 1207	603. Aug. 8, 1206.
1129	4308	Prabhava ..	383 — 384	1207 – 1208	604. July 28, 1207.
1130	4309	Vibhava	384 — 385	1208 – 1209	605. July 16, 1208.
1131	4310	Śukla	385 — 386	1209 – 1210	606. July 6, 1209.
1132	4311	Pramodūta ..	386 — 387	1210 – 1211	607. June 25, 1210.
1133	4312	Prajotpatti ..	387 — 388	1211 – 1212	608. June 15, 1211.
1134	4313	Āṅgirasa ..	388 — 389	1212 – 1213	609. June 3, 1212.
1135	4314	Śrīmukha ..	389 — 390	1213 – 1214	610. May 23, 1213.
1136	4315	Bhava	390 — 391	1214 – 1215	611. May 13, 1214.
1137	4316	Yuva	391 — 392	1215 – 1216	612. May 1, 1215.
1138	4317	Dhātu	392 — 393	1216 – 1217	613. April 20, 1216.
1139	4318	Īśvara	393 — 394	1217 – 1218	614. April 10, 1217.
1140	4319	Bahudhānya ..	394 — 395	1218 – 1219	615. March 30, 1218.
1141	4320	Pramādhi ..	395 — 396	1219 – 1220	616. March 19, 1219.
1142	4321	Vikrama	396 — 397	1220 – 1221	617. March 8, 1220.
1143	4322	Vishu, or Vṛishu.	397 — 398	1221 – 1222	618. Feb. 25, 1221.
1144	4323	Chitrabhānu ..	398 — 399	1222 – 1223	619. Feb. 15, 1222.

Year of the *Śālivāhana Śaka.*	Year of the *Kaliyuga.*	Cyclic Year.	*Kollam Āṇḍu*, or Era of Quilon.	Christian Era (A.D.)	The *Hijra* Year commences.
1145	4324	Subhānu ..	399 — 400	1223 – 1224	620. Feb. 4, 1223.
1146	4325	Tāraṇa	400 — 401	1224 – 1225	621. Jan. 24, 1224.
1147	4326	Pārthiva	401 — 402	1225 – 1226	622. Jan. 13, 1225.
1148	4327	Vyaya	402 — 403	1226 – 1227	623. Jan. 2, 1226.
1149	4328	Sarvajit	403 — 404	1227 – 1228	624. Dec. 22, 1226. 625. Dec. 13, 1227.
1150	4329	Sarvadhāri ..	404 — 405	1228 – 1229	626. Nov. 30, 1228.
1151	4330	Virodhi	405 — 406	1229 – 1230	627. Nov. 20, 1229.
1152	4331	Vikṛiti	406 — 407	1230 – 1231	628. Nov. 9, 1230.
1153	4332	Khara	407 — 408	1231 – 1232	629. Oct. 29, 1231.
1154	4333	Nandana ..	408 — 409	1232 – 1233	630. Oct. 18, 1232.
1155	4334	Vijaya	409 — 410	1233 – 1234	631. Oct. 7, 1233.
1156	4335	Jaya	410 — 411	1234 – 1235	632. Sept. 26, 1234.
1157	4336	Manmadha ..	411 — 412	1235 – 1236	633. Sept. 16, 1235.
1158	4337	Durmukhi ..	412 — 413	1236 – 1237	634. Sept. 4, 1236.
1159	4338	Hevilaṁbi ..	413 — 414	1237 – 1238	635. Aug. 24, 1237.
1160	4339	Vilaṁbi	414 — 415	1238 – 1239	636. Aug. 14, 1238.
1161	4340	Vikāri	415 — 416	1239 – 1240	637. Aug. 3, 1239.
1162	4341	Śārvari	416 — 417	1240 – 1241	638. July 23, 1240.
1163	4342	Plava	417 — 418	1241 – 1242	639. July 12, 1241.
1164	4343	Śubhakṛit ..	418 — 419	1242 – 1243	640. July 1, 1242.
1165	4344	Śobhana, or -kṛit.	419 — 420	1243 – 1244	641. June 21, 1243.
1166	4345	Krodhi	420 — 421	1244 – 1245	642. June 9, 1244.
1167	4346	Viśvāvasu ..	421 — 422	1245 – 1246	643. May 29, 1245.
1168	4347	Parābhava ..	422 — 423	1246 – 1247	644. May 19, 1246.
1169	4348	Plavaṅga ..	423 — 424	1247 – 1248	645. May 8, 1247.
1170	4349	Kīlaka	424 — 425	1248 – 1249	646. April 26, 1248.
1171	4350	Saumya	425 — 426	1249 – 1250	647. April 16, 1249.
1172	4351	Sādhāraṇa ..	426 — 427	1250 – 1251	648. April 5, 1250.
1173	4352	Virodhikṛit ..	427 — 428	1251 – 1252	649. March 26, 1251.
1174	4353	Parīdhāvi, or -pi.	428 — 429	1252 – 1253	650. March 14, 1252.
1175	4354	Pramādīcha ..	429 — 430	1253 – 1254	651. March 3, 1253.
1176	4355	Ānanda	430 — 431	1254 – 1255	652. Feb. 21, 1254.
1177	4356	Rākshasa ..	431 — 432	1255 – 1256	653. Feb. 10, 1255.
1178	4357	Nala	432 — 433	1256 – 1257	654. Jan. 30, 1256.
1179	4358	Piṅgala	433 — 434	1257 – 1258	655. Jan. 19, 1257.
1180	4359	Kālayukti ..	434 — 435	1258 – 1259	656. Jan. 8, 1258.
1181	4360	Siddhārthi ..	435 — 436	1259 – 1260	657. Dec. 29, 1258. 658. Dec. 18, 1259.

Year of the *Śālivāhana Śaka.*	Year of the *Kaliyuga.*	Cyclic Year.	*Kollam Āṇḍu*, or Era of Quilon.	Christian Era (A.D.)	The *Hijra* Year commences.
1182	4361	Raudri	436 — 437	1260 — 1261	659. Dec. 6, 1260.
1183	4362	Durmati	437 — 438	1261 — 1262	660. Nov. 26, 1261.
1184	4363	Dundubhi	438 — 439	1262 — 1263	661. Nov. 15, 1262.
1185	4364	Rudhirodgāri	439 — 440	1263 — 1264	662. Nov. 1, 1263.
1186	4365	Raktākshi	440 — 441	1264 — 1265	663. Oct. 24, 1264.
1187	4366	Krodhana	441 — 442	1265 — 1266	664. Oct. 13, 1265.
1188	4367	Akshaya	442 — 443	1266 — 1267	665. Oct. 2, 1266.
1189	4368	Prabhava	443 — 444	1267 — 1268	666. Sept. 22, 1267.
1190	4369	Vibhava	444 — 445	1268 — 1269	667. Sept. 10, 1268.
1191	4370	Śukla	445 — 446	1269 — 1270	668. Aug. 31, 1269.
1192	4371	Pramodūta	446 — 447	1270 — 1271	669. Aug. 20, 1270.
1193	4372	Prajotpatti	447 — 448	1271 — 1272	670. Aug. 9, 1271.
1194	4373	Āṅgirasa	448 — 449	1272 — 1273	671. July 29, 1272.
1195	4374	Śrīmukha	449 — 450	1273 — 1274	672. July 18, 1273.
1196	4375	Bhava	450 — 451	1274 — 1275	673. July 7, 1274.
1197	4376	Yuva	451 — 452	1275 — 1276	674. June 27, 1275.
1198	4377	Dhātu	452 — 453	1276 — 1277	675. June 15, 1276.
1199	4378	Īśvara	453 — 454	1277 — 1278	676. June 4, 1277.
1200	4379	Bahudhānya	454 — 455	1278 — 1279	677. May 25, 1278.
1201	4380	Pramādhi	455 — 456	1279 — 1280	678. May 14, 1279.
1202	4381	Vikrama	456 — 457	1280 — 1281	679. May 3, 1280.
1203	4382	Vishu, or Vṛishu.	457 — 458	1281 — 1282	680. April 22, 1281.
1204	4383	Chitrabhānu	458 — 459	1282 — 1283	681. April 11, 1282.
1205	4384	Subhānu	459 — 460	1283 — 1284	682. April 1, 1283.
1206	4385	Tāraṇa	460 — 461	1284 — 1285	683. March 20, 1284.
1207	4386	Pārthiva	461 — 462	1285 — 1286	684. March 9, 1285.
1208	4387	Vyaya	462 — 463	1286 — 1287	685. Feb. 27, 1286.
1209	4388	Sarvajit	463 — 464	1287 — 1288	686. Feb. 16, 1287.
1210	4389	Sarvadhāri	464 — 465	1288 — 1289	687. Feb. 6, 1288.
1211	4390	Virodhi	465 — 466	1289 — 1290	688. Jan. 25, 1289.
1212	4391	Vikṛiti	466 — 467	1290 — 1291	689. Jan. 14, 1290.
1213	4392	Khara	467 — 468	1291 — 1292	690. Jan. 4, 1291.
1214	4393	Nandana	468 — 469	1292 — 1293	691. Dec. 24, 1291. 692. Dec. 12, 1292.
1215	4394	Vijaya	469 — 470	1293 — 1294	693. Dec. 2, 1293.
1216	4395	Jaya	470 — 471	1294 — 1295	694. Nov. 21, 1294.
1217	4396	Manmadha	471 — 472	1295 — 1296	695. Nov. 10, 1295.
1218	4397	Durmukhi	472 — 473	1296 — 1297	696. Oct. 30, 1296.
1219	4398	Hevilaṁbi	473 — 474	1297 — 1298	697. Oct. 19, 1297.

Year of the *Sâlivâhana Śaka.*	Year of the *Kaliyuga.*	Cyclic Year.	*Kollam Āndu*, or Era of Quilon.	Christian Era (A.D.)	The *Hijra* Year commences.
1220	4399	Vilambi	474 — 475	1298 — 1299	698. Oct. 8, 1298.
1221	4400	Vikāri	475 — 476	1299 — 1300	699. Sept. 28, 1299.
1222	4401	Śārvari	476 — 477	1300 — 1301	700. Sept. 16, 1300.
1223	4402	Plava	477 — 478	1301 — 1302	701. Sept. 6, 1301.
1224	4403	Śubhakṛit ..	478 — 479	1302 — 1303	702. Aug. 26, 1302.
1225	4404	Śobhana, or -kṛit.	479 — 480	1303 — 1304	703. Aug. 15, 1303.
1226	4405	Krodhi	480 — 481	1304 — 1305	704. Aug. 4, 1304.
1227	4406	Viśvāvasu ..	481 — 482	1305 — 1306	705. July 24, 1305.
1228	4407	Parābhava ..	482 — 483	1306 — 1307	706. July 13, 1306.
1229	4408	Plavaṅga ..	483 — 484	1307 — 1308	707. July 3, 1307.
1230	4409	Kīlaka	484 — 485	1308 — 1309	708. June 21, 1308.
1231	4410	Saumya	485 — 486	1309 — 1310	709. June 11, 1309.
1232	4411	Sādhāraṇa ..	486 — 487	1310 — 1311	710. May 31, 1310.
1233	4412	Virodhikṛit ..	487 — 488	1311 — 1312	711. May 20, 1311.
1234	4413	Parīdhāvi, or -pi.	488 — 489	1312 — 1313	712. May 9, 1312.
1235	4414	Pramādīcha ..	489 — 490	1313 — 1314	713. April 28, 1313.
1236	4415	Ānanda	490 — 491	1314 — 1315	714. April 17, 1314.
1237	4416	Rākshasa ..	491 — 492	1315 — 1316	715. April 7, 1315.
1238	4417	Nala	492 — 493	1316 — 1317	716. March 26, 1316.
1239	4418	Piṅgala	493 — 494	1317 — 1318	717. March 16, 1317.
1240	4419	Kālayukti ..	494 — 495	1318 — 1319	718. March 5, 1318.
1241	4420	Siddhārthi ..	495 — 496	1319 — 1320	719. Feb. 22, 1319.
1242	4421	Raudri	496 — 497	1320 — 1321	720. Feb. 12, 1320.
1243	4422	Durmati	497 — 498	1321 — 1322	721. Jan. 31, 1321.
1244	4423	Dundubhi ..	498 — 499	1322 — 1323	722. Jan. 20, 1322.
1245	4424	Rudhirodgāri ..	499 — 500	1323 — 1324	723. Jan. 10, 1323.
1246	4425	Raktākshi ..	500 — 501	1324 — 1325	724. Dec. 30, 1323. 725. Dec. 18, 1324.
1247	4426	Krodhana ..	501 — 502	1325 — 1326	726. Dec. 8, 1325.
1248	4427	Akshaya	502 — 503	1326 — 1327	727. Nov. 27, 1326.
1249	4428	Prabhava ..	503 — 504	1327 — 1328	728. Nov. 17, 1327.
1250	4429	Vibhava	504 — 505	1328 — 1329	729. Nov. 5, 1328.
1251	4430	Śukla	505 — 506	1329 — 1330	730. Oct. 25, 1329.
1252	4431	Pramodūta ..	506 — 507	1330 — 1331	731. Oct. 15, 1330.
1253	4432	Prajotpatti ..	507 — 508	1331 — 1332	732. Oct. 4, 1331.
1254	4433	Āṅgirasa ..	508 — 509	1332 — 1333	733. Sept. 22, 1332.
1255	4434	Śrīmukha ..	509 — 510	1333 — 1334	734. Sept. 12, 1333.
1256	4435	Bhava	510 — 511	1334 — 1335	735. Sept. 1, 1334.
1257	4436	Yuva	511 — 512	1335 — 1336	736. Aug. 21, 1335.

Year of the *Śālivāhana Śaka.*	Year of the *Kaliyuga.*	Cyclic Year.	*Kollaṁ Āṇḍu*, or Era of Quilon.	Christian Era (A.D.)	The *Hijra* Year commences.
1258	4437	Dhātu	512 — 513	1336 – 1337	737. Aug. 10, 1336.
1259	4438	Īśvara	513 — 514	1337 – 1338	738. July 30, 1337.
1260	4439	Bahudhānya ..	514 — 515	1338 – 1339	739. July 20, 1338.
1261	4440	Pramādhi ..	515 — 516	1339 – 1340	740. July 9, 1339.
1262	4441	Vikrama	516 — 517	1340 – 1341	741. June 27, 1340.
1263	4442	Vishu, or Vṛishu.	517 — 518	1341 – 1342	742. June 17, 1341.
1264	4443	Chitrabhānu ..	518 — 519	1342 – 1343	743. June 5, 1342.
1265	4444	Subhānu	519 — 520	1343 – 1344	744. May 26, 1343.
1266	4445	Tāraṇa	520 — 521	1344 – 1345	745. May 15, 1344.
1267	4446	Pārthiva	521 — 522	1345 – 1346	746. May 4, 1345.
1268	4447	Vyaya	522 — 523	1346 – 1347	747. April 24, 1346.
1269	4448	Sarvajit	523 — 524	1347 – 1348	748. April 13, 1347.
1270	4449	Sarvadhāri ..	524 — 525	1348 – 1349	749. April 1, 1348.
1271	4450	Virodhi	525 — 526	1349 – 1350	750. March 22, 1349.
1272	4451	Vikṛiti	526 — 527	1350 – 1351	751. March 11, 1350.
1273	4452	Khara	527 — 528	1351 – 1352	752. Feb. 28, 1351.
1274	4453	Nandana ..	528 — 529	1352 – 1353	753. Feb. 18, 1352.
1275	4454	Vijaya	529 — 530	1353 – 1354	754. Feb. 6, 1353.
1276	4455	Jaya.	530 — 531	1354 – 1355	755. Jan. 26, 1354.
1277	4456	Manmadha ..	531 — 532	1355 – 1356	756. Jan. 16, 1355.
1278	4457	Durmukhi ..	532 — 533	1356 – 1357	757. Jan. 5, 1356.
1279	4458	Hevilaṁbi ..	533 — 534	1357 – 1358	758. Dec. 25, 1356. 759. Dec. 14, 1357.
1280	4459	Vilaṁbi	534 — 535	1358 – 1359	760. Dec. 3, 1358.
1281	4460	Vikāri	535 — 536	1359 – 1360	761. Nov. 23, 1359.
1282	4461	Śārvari	536 — 537	1360 – 1361	762. Nov. 11, 1360.
1283	4462	Plava	537 — 538	1361 – 1362	763. Oct. 31, 1361.
1284	4463	Śubhakṛit ..	538 — 539	1362 – 1363	764. Oct. 21, 1362.
1285	4464	Śobhana, or -kṛit.	539 — 540	1363 – 1364	765. Oct. 10, 1363.
1286	4465	Krodhi	540 — 541	1364 – 1365	766. Sept. 28, 1364.
1287	4466	Viśvāvasu ..	541 — 542	1365 – 1366	767. Sept. 18, 1365.
1288	4467	Parābhava ..	542 — 543	1366 – 1367	768. Sept. 7, 1366.
1289	4468	Plavaṅga ..	543 — 544	1367 – 1368	769. Aug. 28, 1367.
1290	4469	Kīlaka	544 — 545	1368 – 1369	770. Aug. 16, 1368.
1291	4470	Saumya	545 — 546	1369 – 1370	771. Aug. 5, 1369.
1292	4471	Sādhāraṇa ..	546 — 547	1370 – 1371	772. July 26, 1370.
1293	4472	Virodhikṛit ..	547 — 548	1371 – 1372	773. July 15, 1371.
1294	4473	Parīdhāvi, or -pi.	548 — 549	1372 – 1373	774. July 3, 1372.
1295	4474	Pramādīcha ..	549 — 550	1373 – 1374	775. June 23, 1373.

Year of the *Śálivdhana Śaka.*	Year of the *Kaliyuga.*	Cyclic Year.	*Kollam Āṇḍu*, or Era of Quilon.	Christian Era (A.D.)	The *Hijra* Year commences.
1296	4475	Ānanda ..	550 — 551	1374 – 1375	776. June 12, 1374.
1297	4476	Rākshasa ..	551 — 552	1375 – 1376	777. June 2, 1375.
1298	4477	Nala	552 — 553	1376 – 1377	778. May 21, 1376.
1299	4478	Piṅgala	553 — 554	1377 – 1378	779. May 10, 1377.
1300	4479	Kālayukti ..	554 — 555	1378 – 1379	780. April 30, 1378.
1301	4480	Siddhārthi ..	555 — 556	1379 – 1380	781. April 19, 1379.
1302	4481	Raudri	556 — 557	1380 – 1381	782. April 7, 1380.
1303	4482	Durmati ..	557 — 558	1381 – 1382	783. March 28, 1381.
1304	4483	Dundubhi ..	558 — 559	1382 – 1383	784. March 17, 1382.
1305	4484	Rudhirodgāri ..	559 — 560	1383 – 1384	785. March 6, 1383.
1306	4485	Raktākshi ..	560 — 561	1384 – 1385	786. Feb. 24, 1384.
1307	4486	Krodhana ..	561 — 562	1385 – 1386	787. Feb. 12, 1385.
1308	4487	Akshaya	562 — 563	1386 – 1387	788. Feb. 2, 1386.
1309	4488	Prabhava ..	563 — 564	1387 – 1388	789. Jan. 22, 1387.
1310	4489	Vibhava ..	564 — 565	1388 – 1389	790. Jan. 11, 1388.
1311	4490	Śukla	565 — 566	1389 – 1390	791. Dec. 31, 1388. 792. Dec. 20, 1389.
1312	4491	Pramodūta ..	566 — 567	1390 – 1391	793. Dec. 9, 1390.
1313	4492	Prajotpatti ..	567 — 568	1391 – 1392	794. Nov. 29, 1391.
1314	4493	Āṅgirasa ..	568 — 569	1392 – 1393	795. Nov. 17, 1392.
1315	4494	Śrīmukha ..	569 — 570	1393 – 1394	796. Nov. 6, 1393.
1316	4495	Bhava	570 — 571	1394 – 1395	797. Oct. 27, 1394.
1317	4496	Yuva	571 — 572	1395 – 1396	798. Oct. 16, 1395.
1318	4497	Dhātu	572 — 573	1396 – 1397	799. Oct. 5, 1396.
1319	4498	Īśvara	573 — 574	1397 – 1398	800. Sept. 24, 1397.
1320	4499	Bahudhānya ..	574 — 575	1398 – 1399	801. Sept. 13, 1398.
1321	4500	Pramādhi ..	575 — 576	1399 – 1400	802. Sept. 3, 1399.
1322	4501	Vikrama ..	576 — 577	1400 – 1401	803. Aug. 22, 1400.
1323	4502	Vishu, or Vṛishu.	577 — 578	1401 – 1402	804. Aug. 11, 1401.
1324	4503	Chitrabhānu ..	578 — 579	1402 – 1403	805. Aug. 1, 1402.
1325	4504	Subhānu ..	579 — 580	1403 – 1404	806. July 21, 1403.
1326	4505	Tāraṇa	580 — 581	1404 – 1405	807. July 10, 1404.
1327	4506	Pārthiva	581 — 582	1405 – 1406	808. June 29, 1405.
1328	4507	Vyaya	582 — 583	1406 – 1407	809. June 18, 1406.
1329	4508	Sarvajit	583 — 584	1407 – 1408	810. June 8, 1407.
1330	4509	Sarvadhāri ..	584 — 585	1408 – 1409	811. May 27, 1408.
1331	4510	Virodhi	585 — 586	1409 – 1410	812. May 16, 1409.
1332	4511	Vikṛiti	586 — 587	1410 – 1411	813. May 6, 1410.
1333	4512	Khara	587 — 588	1411 – 1412	814. April 25, 1411.

Year of the *Śâlivâhana Śaka*.	Year of the *Kaliyuga*.	Cyclic Year.	*Kollam Āṇḍu*, or Era of Quilon.	Christian Era (A.D.)	The *Hijra* Year commences.
1334	4513	Nandana ..	588 — 589	1412 – 1413	815. April 13, 1412.
1335	4514	Vijaya	589 — 590	1413 – 1414	816. April 3, 1413.
1336	4515	Jaya	590 — 591	1414 – 1415	817. March 23, 1414.
1337	4516	Manmadha ..	591 — 592	1415 – 1416	818. March 13, 1415.
1338	4517	Durmukhi ..	592 — 593	1416 – 1417	819. March 1, 1416.
1339	4518	Hevilambi ..	593 — 594	1417 – 1418	820. Feb. 18, 1417.
1340	4519	Vilaṁbi ..	594 — 595	1418 – 1419	821. Feb. 8, 1418.
1341	4520	Vikāri	595 — 596	1419 – 1420	822. Jan. 28, 1419.
1342	4521	Śārvari	596 — 597	1420 – 1421	823. Jan. 17, 1420.
1343	4522	Plava	597 — 598	1421 – 1422	824. Jan. 6, 1421.
1344	4523	Śubhakṛit ..	598 — 599	1422 – 1423	825. Dec. 26, 1421. 826. Dec. 15, 1422.
1345	4524	Śobhana, or -kṛit.	599 — 600	1423 – 1424	827. Dec. 5, 1423.
1346	4525	Krodhi	600 — 601	1424 – 1425	828. Nov. 23, 1424.
1347	4526	Viśvāvasu ..	601 — 602	1425 – 1426	829. Nov. 13, 1425.
1348	4527	Parābhava ..	602 — 603	1426 – 1427	830. Nov. 2, 1426.
1349	4528	Plavaṅga ..	603 — 604	1427 – 1428	831. Oct. 22, 1427.
1350	4529	Kīlaka	604 — 605	1428 – 1429	832. Oct. 11, 1428.
1351	4530	Saumya	605 — 606	1429 – 1430	833. Sept. 30, 1429.
1352	4531	Sādhāraṇa ..	606 — 607	1430 – 1431	834. Sept. 19, 1430.
1353	4532	Virodhikṛit ..	607 — 608	1431 – 1432	835. Sept. 9, 1431.
1354	4533	Parīdhāvi, or -pi.	608 — 609	1432 – 1433	836. Aug. 28, 1432.
1355	4534	Pramādīcha ..	609 — 610	1433 – 1434	837. Aug. 18, 1433.
1356	4535	Ānanda	610 — 611	1434 – 1435	838. Aug. 7, 1434.
1357	4536	Rākshasa ..	611 — 612	1435 – 1436	839. July 27, 1435.
1358	4537	Nala	612 — 613	1436 – 1437	840. July 16, 1436.
1359	4538	Piṅgala	613 — 614	1437 – 1438	841. July 5, 1437.
1360	4539	Kālayukti ..	614 — 615	1438 – 1439	842. June 24, 1438.
1361	4540	Siddhārthi ..	615 — 616	1439 – 1440	843. June 14, 1439.
1362	4541	Raudri	616 — 617	1440 – 1441	844. June 2, 1440.
1363	4542	Durmati ..	617 — 618	1441 – 1442	845. May 22, 1441.
1364	4543	Dundubhi ..	618 — 619	1442 – 1443	846. May 12, 1442.
1365	4544	Rudhirodgāri ..	619 — 620	1443 – 1444	847. May 1, 1443.
1366	4545	Raktākshi ..	620 — 621	1444 – 1445	848. April 20, 1444.
1367	4546	Krodhana ..	621 — 622	1445 – 1446	849. April 9, 1445.
1368	4547	Akshaya ..	622 — 623	1446 – 1447	850. March 29, 1446.
1369	4548	Prabhava ..	623 — 624	1447 – 1448	851. March 19, 1447.
1370	4549	Vibhava ..	624 — 625	1448 – 1449	852. March 7, 1448.
1371	4550	Śukla	625 — 626	1449 – 1450	853. Feb. 24, 1449.

Year of the *Śâlivâhana Śaka.*	Year of the *Kaliyuga.*	Cyclic Year.	*Kollam Āṇḍu*, or Era of Quilon.	Christian Era (A.D.)	The *Hijra* Year commences.
1372	4551	Pramodûta ..	626 — 627	1450 – 1451	854. Feb. 14, 1450.
1373	4552	Prajotpatti ..	627 — 628	1451 – 1452	855. Feb. 3, 1451.
1374	4553	Āṅgirasa ..	628 — 629	1452 – 1453	856. Jan. 23, 1452.
1375	4554	Śrîmukha ..	629 — 630	1453 – 1454	857. Jan. 12, 1453.
1376	4555	Bhava	630 — 631	1454 – 1455	858. Jan. 1, 1454.
1377	4556	Yuva	631 — 632	1455 – 1456	859. Dec. 22, 1454. 860. Dec. 11, 1455.
1378	4557	Dhâtu	632 — 633	1456 – 1457	861. Nov. 29, 1456.
1379	4558	Îśvara	533 — 634	1457 – 1458	862. Nov. 19, 1457.
1380	4559	Bahudhânya ..	634 — 635	1458 – 1459	863. Nov. 8, 1458.
1381	4560	Pramâdhi ..	635 — 636	1459 – 1460	864. Oct. 28, 1459.
1382	4561	Vikrama	636 — 637	1460 – 1461	865. Oct. 17, 1460.
1383	4562	Vishu, or Vṛishu.	637 — 638	1461 – 1462	866. Oct. 6, 1461.
1384	4563	Chitrabhânu ..	638 — 639	1462 – 1463	867. Sept. 26, 1462.
1385	4564	Subhânu ..	639 — 640	1463 – 1464	868. Sept. 15, 1463.
1386	4565	Târaṇa	640 — 641	1464 – 1465	869. Sept. 3, 1464.
1387	4566	Pârthiva ..	641 — 642	1465 – 1466	870. Aug. 24, 1465.
1388	4567	Vyaya	642 — 643	1466 – 1467	871. Aug. 13, 1466.
1389	4568	Sarvajit	643 — 644	1467 – 1468	872. Aug. 2, 1467.
1390	4569	Sarvadhâri ..	644 — 645	1468 – 1469	873. July 22, 1468.
1391	4570	Virodhi	645 — 646	1469 – 1470	874. July 11, 1469.
1392	4571	Vikṛiti	646 — 647	1470 – 1471	875. June 30, 1470.
1393	4572	Khara	647 — 648	1471 – 1472	876. June 19, 1471.
1394	4573	Nandana ..	648 — 649	1472 – 1473	877. June 8, 1472.
1395	4574	Vijaya	649 — 650	1473 – 1474	878. May 29, 1473.
1396	4575	Jaya	650 — 651	1474 – 1475	879. May 18, 1474.
1397	4576	Manmadha ..	651 — 652	1475 – 1476	880. May 7, 1475.
1398	4577	Durmukhi ..	652 — 653	1476 – 1477	881. April 26, 1476.
1399	4578	Hevilambi ..	653 — 654	1477 – 1478	882. April 15, 1477.
1400	4579	Vilambi	654 — 655	1478 – 1479	883. April 4, 1478.
1401	4580	Vikâri	655 — 656	1479 – 1480	884. March 25, 1479.
1402	4581	Śârvari	656 — 657	1480 – 1481	885. March 13, 1480.
1403	4582	Plava	657 — 658	1481 – 1482	886. March 2, 1481.
1404	4583	Śubhakṛit ..	658 — 659	1482 – 1483	887. Feb. 20, 1482.
1405	4584	Śobhana, or -kṛit.	659 — 660	1483 – 1484	888. Feb. 9, 1483.
1406	4585	Krodhi	660 — 661	1484 – 1485	889. Jan. 30, 1484.
1407	4586	Viśvâvasu ..	661 — 662	1485 – 1486	890. Jan. 18, 1485.
1408	4587	Parâbhava ..	662 — 663	1486 – 1487	891. Jan. 7, 1486.
1409	4588	Plavaṅga ..	663 — 664	1487 – 1488	892. Dec. 28, 1486. 893. Dec. 17, 1487.

Year of the *Śālivāhana Śaka*.	Year of the *Kaliyuga*.	Cyclic Year.	*Kollam Āṇḍu*, or Era of Quilon.	Christian Era (A.D.)	The *Hijra* Year commences.
1410	4589	Kīlaka	664 — 665	1488 – 1489	894. Dec. 5, 1488.
1411	4590	Saumya	665 — 666	1489 – 1490	895. Nov. 25, 1489.
1412	4591	Sādhāraṇa ..	666 — 667	1490 – 1491	896. Nov. 14, 1490.
1413	4592	Virodhikṛit ..	667 — 668	1491 – 1492	897. Nov. 4, 1491.
1414	4593	Parīdhāvi, or -pi.	668 — 669	1492 – 1493	898. Oct. 23, 1492.
1415	4594	Pramādīcha ..	669 — 670	1493 – 1494	899. Oct. 12, 1493.
1416	4595	Ānanda	670 — 671	1494 – 1495	900. Oct. 2, 1494.
1417	4596	Rākshasa ..	671 — 672	1495 – 1496	901. Sept. 21, 1495.
1418	4597	Nala	672 — 673	1496 – 1497	902. Sept. 9, 1496.
1419	4598	Piṅgala	673 — 674	1497 – 1498	903. Aug. 30, 1497.
1420	4599	Kālayukti ..	674 — 675	1498 – 1499	904. Aug. 19, 1498.
1421	4600	Siddhārthi ..	675 — 676	1499 – 1500	905. Aug. 8, 1499.
1422	4601	Raudri	676 — 677	1500 – 1501	906. July 28, 1500.
1423	4602	Durmati	677 — 678	1501 – 1502	907. July 17, 1501.
1424	4603	Dundubhi ..	678 — 679	1502 – 1503	908. July 7, 1502.
1425	4604	Rudhirodgāri ..	679 — 680	1503 – 1504	909. June 26, 1503.
1426	4605	Raktākshi ..	680 — 681	1504 – 1505	910. June 14, 1504.
1427	4606	Krodhana ..	681 — 682	1505 – 1506	911. June 4, 1505.
1428	4607	Akshaya	682 — 683	1506 – 1507	912. May 24, 1506.
1429	4608	Prabhava ..	683 — 684	1507 – 1508	913. May 13, 1507.
1430	4609	Vibhava	684 — 685	1508 – 1509	914. May 2, 1508.
1431	4610	Śukla	685 — 686	1509 – 1510	915. April 21, 1509.
1432	4611	Pramodūta ..	686 — 687	1510 – 1511	916. April 10, 1510.
1433	4612	Prajotpatti ..	687 — 688	1511 – 1512	917. March 31, 1511.
1434	4613	Āṅgirasa ..	688 — 689	1512 – 1513	918. March 19, 1512.
1435	4614	Śrīmukha ..	689 — 690	1513 – 1514	919. March 9, 1513.
1436	4615	Bhava	690 — 691	1514 – 1515	920. Feb. 26, 1514.
1437	4616	Yuva	691 — 692	1515 – 1516	921. Feb. 15, 1515.
1438	4617	Dhātu	692 — 693	1516 – 1517	922. Feb. 5, 1516.
1439	4618	Īśvara	693 — 694	1517 – 1518	923. Jan. 24, 1517.
1440	4619	Bahudhānya ..	694 — 695	1518 – 1519	924. Jan. 13, 1518.
1441	4620	Pramādhi ..	695 — 696	1519 – 1520	925. Jan. 3, 1519.
1442	4621	Vikrama	696 — 697	1520 – 1521	{ 926. Dec. 23, 1519. 927. Dec. 12, 1520.
1443	4622	Vishu, or Vṛishu.	697 — 698	1521 – 1522	928. Dec. 1, 1521.
1444	4623	Chitrabhānu ..	698 — 699	1522 – 1523	929. Nov. 20, 1522.
1445	4624	Subhānu	699 — 700	1523 – 1524	930. Nov. 10, 1523.
1446	4625	Tāraṇa	700 — 701	1524 – 1525	931. Oct. 29, 1524.
1447	4626	Pārthiva	701 — 702	1525 – 1526	932. Oct. 18, 1525.

Year of the *Sâlivâhana Śaka.*	Year of the *Kaliyuga.*	Cyclic Year.	*Kollam Āṇdu*, or Era of Quilon.	Christian Era (A.D.)	The *Hijra* Year commences.
1448	4627	Vyaya	702 — 703	1526 — 1527	933. Oct. 8, 1526.
1449	4628	Sarvajit	703 — 704	1527 — 1528	934. Sept. 27, 1527.
1450	4629	Sarvadhāri ..	704 — 705	1528 — 1529	935. Sept. 15, 1528.
1451	4630	Virodhi	705 — 706	1529 — 1530	936. Sept. 5, 1529.
1452	4631	Vikṛiti	706 — 707	1530 — 1531	937. Aug. 25, 1530.
1453	4632	Khara	707 — 708	1531 — 1532	938. Aug. 15, 1531.
1454	4633	Nandana ..	708 — 709	1532 — 1533	939. Aug. 3, 1532.
1455	4634	Vijaya	709 — 710	1533 — 1534	940. July 23, 1533.
1456	4635	Jaya	710 — 711	1534 — 1535	941. July 13, 1534.
1457	4636	Manmadha ..	711 — 712	1535 — 1536	942. July 2, 1535.
1458	4637	Durmukhi ..	712 — 713	1536 — 1537	943. June 20, 1536.
1459	4638	Hevilambi ..	713 — 714	1537 — 1538	944. June 10, 1537.
1460	4639	Vilambi	714 — 715	1538 — 1539	945. May 30, 1538.
1461	4640	Vikāri	715 — 716	1539 — 1540	946. May 19, 1539.
1462	4641	Śārvari	716 — 717	1540 — 1541	947. May 8, 1540.
1463	4642	Plava	717 — 718	1541 — 1542	948. April 27, 1541.
1464	4643	Śubhakṛit ..	718 — 719	1542 — 1543	949. April 17, 1542.
1465	4644	Śobhana, or -kṛit.	719 — 720	1543 — 1544	950. April 6, 1543.
1466	4645	Krodhi	720 — 721	1544 — 1545	951. March 25, 1544.
1467	4646	Viśvāvasu ..	721 — 722	1545 — 1546	952. March 15, 1545
1468	4647	Parābhava ..	722 — 723	1546 — 1547	953. March 4, 1546.
1469	4648	Plavaṅga ..	723 — 724	1547 — 1548	954. Feb. 21, 1547.
1470	4649	Kīlaka	724 — 725	1548 — 1549	955. Feb. 11, 1548.
1471	4650	Saumya	725 — 726	1549 — 1550	956. Jan. 30, 1549.
1472	4651	Sādhāraṇa ..	726 — 727	1550 — 1551	957. Jan. 20, 1550.
1473	4652	Virodhikṛit ..	727 — 728	1551 — 1552	958. Jan. 9, 1551.
1474	4653	Parīdhāvi, or -pi.	728 — 729	1552 — 1553	959. Dec. 29, 1551. 960. Dec. 18, 1552.
1475	4654	Pramādīcha ..	729 — 730	1553 — 1554	961. Dec. 7, 1553.
1476	4655	Ānanda	730 — 731	1554 — 1555	962. Nov. 26, 1554.
1477	4656	Rākshasa ..	731 — 732	1555 — 1556	963. Nov. 16, 1555.
1478	4657	Nala	732 — 733	1556 — 1557	964. Nov. 4, 1556.
1479	4658	Piṅgala	733 — 734	1557 — 1558	965. Oct. 24, 1557.
1480	4659	Kālayukti ..	734 — 735	1558 — 1559	966. Oct. 14, 1558.
1481	4660	Siddhārthi ..	735 — 736	1559 — 1560	967. Oct. 3, 1559.
1482	4661	Raudri	736 — 737	1560 — 1561	968. Sept. 22, 1560.
1483	4662	Durmati	737 — 738	1561 — 1562	969. Sept. 11, 1561.
1484	4663	Dundubhi ..	738 — 739	1562 — 1563	970. Aug. 31, 1562.
1485	4664	Rudhirodgāri ..	739 — 740	1563 — 1564	971. Aug. 21, 1563.

Year of the *Śālivāhana Śaka.*	Year of the *Kaliyuga.*	Cyclic Year.	*Kollam Āṇḍu*, or Era of Quilon.	Christian Era (A.D.)	The *Hijra* Year commences.
1486	4665	Raktākshi ..	740 — 741	1564 – 1565	972. Aug. 9, 1564.
1487	4666	Krodhana ..	741 — 742	1565 – 1566	973. July 29, 1565.
1488	4667	Akshaya	742 — 743	1566 – 1567	974. July 19, 1566.
1489	4668	Prabhava ..	743 — 744	1567 – 1568	975. July 8, 1567.
1490	4669	Vibhava	744 — 745	1568 – 1569	976. June 26, 1568.
1491	4670	Śukla	745 — 746	1569 – 1570	977. June 16, 1569.
1492	4671	Pramodūta ..	746 — 747	1570 – 1571	978. June 5, 1570.
1493	4672	Prajotpatti ..	747 — 748	1571 – 1572	979. May 26, 1571.
1494	4673	Āṅgirasa ..	748 — 749	1572 – 1573	980. May 14, 1572.
1495	4674	Śrīmukha ..	749 — 750	1573 – 1574	981. May 3, 1573.
1496	4675	Bhava	750 — 751	1574 – 1575	982. April 23, 1574.
1497	4676	Yuva	751 — 752	1575 – 1576	983. April 12, 1575.
1498	4677	Dhātu	752 — 753	1576 – 1577	984. March 31, 1576.
1499	4678	Īśvara	753 — 754	1577 – 1578	985. March 21, 1577.
1500	4679	Bahudhānya ..	754 — 755	1578 – 1579	986. March 10, 1578.
1501	4680	Pramādhi ..	755 — 756	1579 – 1580	987. Feb. 28, 1579.
1502	4681	Vikrama	756 — 757	1580 – 1581	988. Feb. 17, 1580.
1503	4682	Vishu, or Vṛishu.	757 — 758	1581 – 1582	989. Feb. 5, 1581.
1504	4683	Chitrabhānu ..	758 — 759	1582 – 1583	990. Jan. 26, 1582.
1505	4684	Subhānu	759 — 760	1583 – 1584	991. Jan. 15, 1583.
1506	4685	Tāraṇa	760 — 761	1584 – 1585	992. Jan. 4, 1584.
1507	4686	Pārthiva	761 — 762	1585 – 1586	993. Dec. 24, 1584. 994. Dec. 13, 1585.
1508	4687	Vyaya	762 — 763	1586 – 1587	995. Dec. 2, 1586.
1509	4688	Sarvajit	763 — 764	1587 – 1588	996. Nov. 22, 1587.
1510	4689	Sarvadhāri ..	764 — 765	1588 – 1589	997. Nov. 10, 1588.
1511	4690	Virodhi	765 — 766	1589 – 1590	998. Oct. 31, 1589.
1512	4691	Vikṛiti	766 — 767	1590 – 1591	999. Oct. 20, 1590.
1513	4692	Khara	767 — 768	1591 – 1592	1000. Oct. 9, 1591.
1514	4693	Nandana ..	768 — 769	1592 – 1593	1001. Sept. 28, 1592.
1515	4694	Vijaya	769 — 770	1593 – 1594	1002. Sept. 17, 1593.
1516	4695	Jaya	770 — 771	1594 – 1595	1003. Sept. 6, 1594.
1517	4696	Manmadha ..	771 — 772	1595 – 1596	1004. Aug. 27, 1595.
1518	4697	Durmukhi ..	772 — 773	1596 – 1597	1005. Aug. 15, 1596.
1519	4698	Hevilambi ..	773 — 774	1597 – 1598	1006. Aug. 4, 1597.
1520	4699	Vilambi	774 — 775	1598 – 1599	1007. July 25, 1598.
1521	4700	Vikāri	775 — 776	1599 – 1600	1008. July 14, 1599.
1522	4701	Śārvari	776 — 777	1600 – 1601	1009. July 3, 1600.
1523	4702	Plava	777 — 778	1601 – 1602	1010. June 22, 1601.

Year of the *Śālivāhana Śaka.*	Year of the *Kaliyuga.*	Cyclic Year.	*Kollam Āṇḍu*, or Era of Quilon.	Christian Era (A.D.)	The *Hijra* Year commences.
1524	4703	Śubhakṛit ..	778 — 779	1602 – 1603	1011. June 11, 1602.
1525	4704	Śobhana, or -kṛit.	779 — 780	1603 – 1604	1012. June 1, 1603.
1526	4705	Krodhi	780 — 781	1604 – 1605	1013. May 20, 1604.
1527	4706	Viśvāvasu ..	781 — 782	1605 – 1606	1014. May 9, 1605.
1528	4707	Parābhava ..	782 — 783	1606 – 1607	1015. April 29, 1606.
1529	4708	Plavaṅga ..	783 — 784	1607 – 1608	1016. April 18, 1607.
1530	4709	Kīlaka	784 — 785	1608 – 1609	1017. April 7, 1608.
1531	4710	Saumya	785 — 786	1609 – 1610	1018. March 27, 1609.
1532	4711	Sādhāraṇa ..	786 — 787	1610 – 1611	1019. March 16, 1610.
1533	4712	Virodhikṛit ..	787 — 788	1611 – 1612	1020. March 5, 1611.
1534	4713	Parīdhāvi, or -pi.	788 — 789	1612 – 1613	1021. Feb. 23, 1612.
1535	4714	Pramādīcha ..	789 — 790	1613 – 1614	1022. Feb. 11, 1613.
1536	4715	Ānanda	790 — 791	1614 – 1615	1023. Feb. 1, 1614.
1537	4716	Rākshasa ..	791 — 792	1615 – 1616	1024. Jan. 21, 1615.
1538	4717	Nala	792 — 793	1616 – 1617	1025. Jan. 10, 1616.
1539	4718	Piṅgala	793 — 794	1617 – 1618	{ 1026. Dec. 30, 1616. 1027. Dec. 19, 1617.
1540	4719	Kālayukti ..	794 — 795	1618 – 1619	1028. Dec. 9, 1618.
1541	4720	Siddhārthi ..	795 — 796	1619 – 1620	1029. Nov. 28, 1619.
1542	4721	Raudri	796 — 797	1620 – 1621	1030. Nov. 16, 1620.
1543	4722	Durmati	797 — 798	1621 – 1622	1031. Nov. 6, 1621.
1544	4723	Dundubhi ..	798 — 799	1622 – 1623	1032. Oct. 26, 1622.
1545	4724	Rudhirodgāri ..	799 — 800	1623 – 1624	1033. Oct. 15, 1623.
1546	4725	Raktākshi ..	800 — 801	1624 – 1625	1034. Oct. 4, 1624.
1547	4726	Krodhana ..	801 — 802	1625 – 1626	1035. Sept. 23, 1625.
1548	4727	Akshaya	802 — 803	1626 – 1627	1036. Sept. 12, 1626.
1549	4728	Prabhava ..	803 — 804	1627 – 1628	1037. Sept. 2, 1627.
1550	4729	Vibhava	804 — 805	1628 – 1629	1038. Aug. 21, 1628.
1551	4730	Śukla	805 — 806	1629 – 1630	1039. Aug. 11, 1629.
1552	4731	Pramodūta ..	806 — 807	1630 – 1631	1040. July 31, 1630.
1553	4732	Prajotpatti ..	807 — 808	1631 – 1632	1041. July 20, 1631.
1554	4733	Āṅgirasa ..	808 — 809	1632 – 1633	1042. July 9, 1632.
1555	4734	Śrīmukha ..	809 — 810	1633 – 1634	1043. June 28, 1633.
1556	4735	Bhava	810 — 811	1634 – 1635	1044. June 17, 1634.
1557	4736	Yuva	811 — 812	1635 – 1636	1045. June 7, 1635.
1558	4737	Dhātu	812 — 813	1636 – 1637	1046. May 26, 1636.
1559	4738	Īśvara	813 — 814	1637 – 1638	1047. May 16, 1637.
1560	4739	Bahudhānya ..	814 — 815	1638 – 1639	1048. May 5, 1638.
1561	4740	Pramādhi ..	815 — 816	1639 – 1640	1049. April 24, 1639.

Year of the *Śâlivâhana Śaka*.	Year of the *Kaliyuga*.	Cyclic Year.	*Kollam Āṇḍu*, or Era of Quilon.	Christian Era (A.D.)	The *Hijra* Year commences.
1562	4741	Vikrama	816 — 817	1640 – 1641	1050. April 13, 1640.
1563	4742	Vishu, or Vṛishu.	817 — 818	1641 – 1642	1051. April 2, 1641.
1564	4743	Chitrabhānu ..	818 — 819	1642 – 1643	1052. March 22, 1642.
1565	4744	Subhānu	819 — 820	1643 – 1644	1053. March 12, 1643.
1566	4745	Tāraṇa	820 — 821	1644 – 1645	1054. Feb. 29, 1644.
1567	4746	Pārthiva	821 — 822	1645 – 1646	1055. Feb. 17, 1645.
1568	4747	Vyaya	822 — 823	1646 – 1647	1056. Feb. 7, 1646.
1569	4748	Sarvajit	823 — 824	1647 – 1648	1057. Jan. 27, 1647.
1570	4749	Sarvadhāri ..	824 — 825	1648 – 1649	1058. Jan. 17, 1648.
1571	4750	Virodhi	825 — 826	1649 – 1650	1059. Jan. 5, 1649.
1572	4751	Vikṛiti	826 — 827	1650 – 1651	1060. Dec. 25, 1649. 1061. Dec. 15, 1650.
1573	4752	Khara	827 — 828	1651 – 1652	1062. Dec. 4, 1651.
1574	4753	Nandana ..	828 — 829	1652 – 1653	1063. Nov. 22, 1652.
1575	4754	Vijaya	829 — 830	1653 – 1654	1064. Nov. 12, 1653.
1576	4755	Jaya	830 — 831	1654 – 1655	1065. Nov. 1, 1654.
1577	4756	Manmadha ..	831 — 832	1655 – 1656	1066. Oct. 21, 1655.
1578	4757	Durmukhi ..	832 — 833	1656 – 1657	1067. Oct. 10, 1656.
1579	4758	Hevilambi ..	833 — 834	1657 – 1658	1068. Sept. 29, 1657.
1580	4759	Vilambi	834 — 835	1658 – 1659	1069. Sept. 19, 1658.
1581	4760	Vikāri	835 — 836	1659 – 1660	1070. Sept. 8, 1659.
1582	4761	Śārvari	836 — 837	1660 – 1661	1071. Aug. 27, 1660.
1583	4762	Plava	837 — 838	1661 – 1662	1072. Aug. 17, 1661.
1584	4763	Śubhakṛit ..	838 — 839	1662 – 1663	1073. Aug. 6, 1662.
1585	4764	Śobhana, or -kṛit.	839 — 840	1663 – 1664	1074. July 26, 1663.
1586	4765	Krodhi	840 — 841	1664 – 1665	1075. July 15, 1664.
1587	4766	Viśvāvasu ..	841 — 842	1665 – 1666	1076. July 4, 1665.
1588	4767	Parābhava ..	842 — 843	1666 – 1667	1077. June 24, 1666.
1589	4768	Plavaṅga ..	843 — 844	1667 – 1668	1078. June 13, 1667.
1590	4769	Kīlaka	844 — 845	1668 – 1669	1079. June 1, 1668.
1591	4770	Saumya	845 — 846	1669 – 1670	1080. May 22, 1669.
1592	4771	Sādhāraṇa ..	846 — 847	1670 – 1671	1081. May 11, 1670.
1593	4772	Virodhikṛit ..	847 — 848	1671 – 1672	1082. April 30, 1671.
1594	4773	Parīdhāvi, or -pi.	848 — 849	1672 – 1673	1083. April 19, 1672.
1595	4774	Pramādīcha ..	849 — 850	1673 – 1674	1084. April 8, 1673.
1596	4775	Ānanda	850 — 851	1674 – 1675	1085. March 28, 1674.
1597	4776	Rākshasa ..	851 — 852	1675 – 1676	1086. March 18, 1675.
1598	4777	Nala	852 — 853	1676 – 1677	1087. March 6, 1676.
1599	4778	Piṅgala	853 — 854	1677 – 1678	1088. Feb. 24, 1677.

Year of the *Śáliváhana Śaka*.	Year of the *Kaliyuga*.	Cyclic Year.	*Kollam Āṇḍu*, or Era of Quilon.	Christian Era (A.D.)	The *Hijra* Year commences.
1600	4779	Kālayukti ..	854 — 855	1678 – 1679	1089. Feb. 13, 1678.
1601	4780	Siddhārthi ..	855 — 856	1679 – 1680	1090. Feb. 2, 1679.
1602	4781	Raudri	856 — 857	1680 – 1681	1091. Jan. 23, 1680.
1603	4782	Durmati	857 — 858	1681 – 1682	1092. Jan. 11, 1681.
1604	4783	Dundubhi ..	858 — 859	1682 – 1683	1093. Dec. 31, 1681. 1094. Dec. 21, 1682.
1605	4784	Rudhirodgāri ..	859 — 860	1683 – 1684	1095. Dec. 10, 1683.
1606	4785	Raktākshi ..	860 — 861	1684 – 1685	1096. Nov. 28, 1684.
1607	4786	Krodhana ..	861 — 862	1685 – 1686	1097. Nov. 18, 1685.
1608	4787	Akshaya	862 — 863	1686 – 1687	1098. Nov. 7, 1686.
1609	4788	Prabhava ..	863 — 864	1687 – 1688	1099. Oct. 28, 1687.
1610	4789	Vibhava	864 — 865	1688 – 1689	1100. Oct. 16, 1688.
1611	4790	Śukla	865 — 866	1689 – 1690	1101. Oct. 5, 1689.
1612	4791	Pramodūta ..	866 — 867	1690 – 1691	1102. Sept. 25, 1690.
1613	4792	Prajotpatti ..	867 — 868	1691 – 1692	1103. Sept. 14, 1691.
1614	4793	Āṅgirasa ..	868 — 869	1692 – 1693	1104. Sept. 2, 1692.
1615	4794	Śrīmukha ..	869 — 870	1693 – 1694	1105. Aug. 23, 1693.
1616	4795	Bhava	870 — 871	1694 – 1695	1106. Aug. 12, 1694.
1617	4796	Yuva	871 — 872	1695 – 1696	1107. Aug. 2, 1695.
1618	4797	Dhātu	872 — 873	1696 – 1697	1108. July 21, 1696.
1619	4798	Īśvara	873 — 874	1697 – 1698	1109. July 10, 1697.
1620	4799	Bahudhānya ..	874 — 875	1698 – 1699	1110. June 30, 1698.
1621	4800	Pramādhi ..	875 — 876	1699 – 1700	1111. June 19, 1699.
1622	4801	Vikrama	876 — 877	1700 – 1701	1112. June 7, 1700.
1623	4802	Vishu, or Vṛishu.	877 — 878	1701 – 1702	1113. May 28, 1701.
1624	4803	Chitrabhānu ..	878 — 879	1702 – 1703	1114. May 17, 1702.
1625	4804	Subhānu	879 — 880	1703 – 1704	1115. May 6, 1703.
1626	4805	Tāraṇa	880 — 881	1704 – 1705	1116. April 25, 1704.
1627	4806	Pārthiva	881 — 882	1705 – 1706	1117. April 14, 1705.
1628	4807	Vyaya	882 — 883	1706 – 1707	1118. April 4, 1706.
1629	4808	Sarvajit	883 — 884	1707 – 1708	1119. March 24, 1707.
1630	4809	Sarvadhāri ..	884 — 885	1708 – 1709	1120. March 12, 1708.
1631	4810	Virodhi	885 — 886	1709 – 1710	1121. March 2, 1709.
1632	4811	Vikṛiti	886 — 887	1710 – 1711	1122. Feb. 19, 1710.
1633	4812	Khara	887 — 888	1711 – 1712	1123. Feb. 8, 1711.
1634	4813	Nandana ..	888 — 889	1712 – 1713	1124. Jan. 29, 1712.
1635	4814	Vijaya	889 — 890	1713 – 1714	1125. Jan. 17, 1713.
1636	4815	Jaya	890 — 891	1714 – 1715	1126. Jan. 6, 1714.
1637	4816	Manmadha ..	891 — 892	1715 – 1716	1127. Dec. 27, 1714. 1128. Dec. 16, 1715.

Year of the *Śālivāhana Śaka.*	Year of the *Kaliyuga.*	Cyclic Year.	*Kollaṁ Āṇḍu*, or Era of Quilon.	Christian Era (A.D.)	The *Hijra* Year commences.
1638	4817	Durmukhi ..	892 — 893	1716 – 1717	1129. Dec. 5, 1716.
1639	4818	Hevilaṁbi ..	893 — 894	1717 – 1718	1130. Nov. 24, 1717.
1640	4819	Vilaṁbi	894 — 895	1718 – 1719	1131. Nov. 13, 1718.
1641	4820	Vikāri	895 — 896	1719 – 1720	1132. Nov. 3, 1719.
1642	4821	Śārvari	896 — 897	1720 – 1721	1133. Oct. 22, 1720.
1643	4822	Plava	897 — 898	1721 – 1722	1134. Oct. 11, 1721.
1644	4823	Śubhakṛit ..	898 — 899	1722 – 1723	1135. Oct. 1, 1722.
1645	4824	Śobhana, or -kṛit.	899 — 900	1723 – 1724	1136. Sept. 20, 1723.
1646	4825	Krodhi	900 — 901	1724 – 1725	1137. Sept. 9, 1724.
1647	4826	Viśvāvasu ..	901 — 902	1725 – 1726	1138. Aug. 29, 1725.
1648	4827	Parābhava ..	902 — 903	1726 – 1727	1139. Aug. 18, 1726.
1649	4828	Plavaṅga ..	903 — 904	1727 – 1728	1140. Aug. 8, 1727.
1650	4829	Kīlaka	904 — 905	1728 – 1729	1141. July 27, 1728.
1651	4830	Saumya	905 — 906	1729 – 1730	1142. July 16, 1729.
1652	4831	Sādhāraṇa ..	906 — 907	1730 – 1731	1143. July 6, 1730.
1653	4832	Virodhikṛit ..	907 — 908	1731 – 1732	1144. June 25, 1731.
1654	4833	Parīdhāvi, or -pi.	908 — 909	1732 – 1733	1145. June 13, 1732.
1655	4834	Pramādīcha ..	909 — 910	1733 – 1734	1146. June 3, 1733.
1656	4835	Ānanda	910 — 911	1734 – 1735	1147. May 23, 1734.
1657	4836	Rakshasa ..	911 — 912	1735 – 1736	1148. May 13, 1735.
1658	4837	Nala	912 — 913	1736 – 1737	1149. May 1, 1736.
1659	4838	Piṅgala	913 — 914	1737 – 1738	1150. April 20, 1737.
1660	4839	Kālayukti ..	914 — 915	1738 – 1739	1151. April 10, 1738.
1661	4840	Siddhārthi ..	915 — 916	1739 – 1740	1152. March 30, 1739.
1662	4841	Raudri	916 — 917	1740 – 1741	1153. March 18, 1740.
1663	4842	Durmati	917 — 918	1741 – 1742	1154. March 8, 1741.
1664	4843	Dundubhi ..	918 — 919	1742 – 1743	1155. Feb. 25, 1742.
1665	4844	Rudhirodgāri ..	919 — 920	1743 – 1744	1156. Feb. 14, 1743.
1666	4845	Raktākshi ..	920 — 921	1744 – 1745	1157. Feb. 4, 1744.
1667	4846	Krodhana ..	921 — 922	1745 – 1746	1158. Jan. 23, 1745.
1668	4847	Akshaya	922 — 923	1746 – 1747	1159. Jan. 13, 1746.
1669	4848	Prabhava ..	923 — 924	1747 – 1748	1160. Jan. 2, 1747.
1670	4849	Vibhava	924 — 925	1748 – 1749	1161. Dec. 22, 1747. 1162. Dec. 11, 1748.
1671	4850	Śukla	925 — 926	1749 – 1750	1163. Nov. 30, 1749.
1672	4851	Pramodūta ..	926 — 927	1750 – 1751	1164. Nov. 19, 1750.
1673	4852	Prajotpatti ..	927 — 928	1751 – 1752	1165. Nov. 9, 1751.
1674	4853	Āṅgirasa ..	928 — 929	1752 – 1753	1166. Nov. 8, 1752.
1675	4854	Śrīmukha ..	929 — 930	1753 – 1754	1167. Oct. 28, 1753.

Year of the *Śālivāhana Śaka.*	Year of the *Kaliyuga.*	Cyclic Year.	*Kollam Āṇḍu*, or Era of Quilon.	Christian Era (A.D.)	The *Hijra* Year commences.
1676	4855	Bhava	930 — 931	1754 — 1755	1168. Oct. 18, 1754.
1677	4856	Yuva	931 — 932	1755 — 1756	1169. Oct. 8, 1755.
1678	4857	Dhātu	932 — 933	1756 — 1757	1170. Sept. 26, 1756.
1679	4858	Īśvara	933 — 934	1757 — 1758	1171. Sept. 16, 1757.
1680	4859	Bahudhānya ..	934 — 935	1758 — 1759	1172. Sept. 5, 1758.
1681	4860	Pramādhi ..	935 — 936	1759 — 1760	1173. Aug. 25, 1759.
1682	4861	Vikrama	936 — 937	1760 — 1761	1174. Aug. 13, 1760.
1683	4862	Vishu, or Vṛishu.	937 — 938	1761 — 1762	1175. Aug. 3, 1761.
1684	4863	Chitrabhānu ..	938 — 939	1762 — 1763	1176. July 23, 1762.
1685	4864	Subhānu	939 — 940	1763 — 1764	1177. July 13, 1763.
1686	4865	Tāraṇa	940 — 941	1764 — 1765	1178. July 1, 1764.
1687	4866	Pārthiva	941 — 942	1765 — 1766	1179. June 20, 1765.
1688	4867	Vyaya	942 — 943	1766 — 1767	1180. June 10, 1766.
1689	4868	Sarvajit	943 — 944	1767 — 1768	1181. May 30, 1767.
1690	4869	Sarvadhāri ..	944 — 945	1768 — 1769	1182. May 18, 1768.
1691	4870	Virodhi	945 — 946	1769 — 1770	1183. May 8, 1769.
1692	4871	Vikṛiti	946 — 947	1770 — 1771	1184. April 21, 1770.
1693	4872	Khara	947 — 948	1771 — 1772	1185. April 17, 1771.
1694	4873	Nandana ..	948 — 949	1772 — 1773	1186. April 5, 1772.
1695	4874	Vijaya	949 — 950	1773 — 1774	1187. March 25, 1773.
1696	4875	Jaya	950 — 951	1774 — 1775	1188. March 14, 1774.
1697	4876	Manmadha ..	951 — 952	1775 — 1776	1189. March 4, 1775.
1698	4877	Durmukhi ..	952 — 953	1776 — 1777	1190. Feb. 21, 1776.
1699	4878	Hevilambi ..	953 — 954	1777 — 1778	1191. Feb. 10, 1777.
1700	4879	Vilambi	954 — 955	1778 — 1779	1192. Jan. 31, 1778.
1701	4880	Vikāri	955 — 956	1779 — 1780	1193. Jan. 20, 1779.
1702	4881	Śārvari	956 — 957	1780 — 1781	1194. Jan. 9, 1780.
1703	4882	Plava	957 — 958	1781 — 1782	{ 1195. Dec. 28, 1780. 1196. Dec. 17, 1781.
1704	4883	Śubhakṛit ..	958 — 959	1782 — 1783	1197. Dec. 7, 1782.
1705	4884	Śobhana, or -kṛit.	959 — 960	1783 — 1784	1198. Nov. 26, 1783.
1706	4885	Krodhi	960 — 961	1784 — 1785	1199. Nov. 15, 1784.
1707	4886	Viśvāvasu ..	961 — 962	1785 — 1786	1200. Nov. 1, 1785.
1708	4887	Parābhava ..	962 — 963	1786 — 1787	1201. Oct. 24, 1786.
1709	4888	Plavaṅga ..	963 — 964	1787 — 1788	1202. Oct. 13, 1787.
1710	4889	Kīlaka	964 — 965	1788 — 1789	1203. Oct. 2, 1788.
1711	4890	Saumya	965 — 966	1789 — 1790	1204. Sept. 21, 1789.
1712	4891	Sādhāraṇa ..	966 — 967	1790 — 1791	1205. Sept. 11, 1790.
1713	4892	Virodhikṛit ..	967 — 968	1791 — 1792	1206. Aug. 31, 1791.

Year of the *Śālivāhana Śaka.*	Year of the *Kaliyuga.*	Cyclic Year.	*Kollam Āṇḍu*, or Era of Quilon.	Christian Era (A.D.)	The *Hijra* Year commences.
1714	4893	Parīdhāvi, or -pi.	968 — 969	1792 – 1793	1207. Aug. 20, 1792.
1715	4894	Pramādīcha ..	969 — 970	1793 – 1794	1208. Aug. 9, 1793.
1716	4895	Ānanda	970 — 971	1794 – 1795	1209. July 29, 1794.
1717	4896	Rākshasa ..	971 — 972	1795 – 1796	1210. July 18, 1795.
1718	4897	Nala	972 — 973	1796 – 1797	1211. July 7, 1796.
1719	4898	Piṅgala	973 — 974	1797 – 1798	1212. June 27, 1797.
1720	4899	Kālayukti ..	974 — 975	1798 – 1799	1213. June 16, 1798.
1721	4900	Siddhārthi ..	975 — 976	1799 – 1800	1214. June 6, 1799.
1722	4901	Raudri	976 — 977	1800 – 1801	1215. May 26, 1800.
1723	4902	Durmati ..	977 — 978	1801 – 1802	1216. May 15, 1801.
1724	4903	Dundubhi ..	978 — 979	1802 – 1803	1217. May 4, 1802.
1725	4904	Rudhirodgāri ..	979 — 980	1803 – 1804	1218. April 24, 1803.
1726	4905	Raktākshi ..	980 — 981	1804 – 1805	1219. April 12, 1804.
1727	4906	Krodhana ..	981 — 982	1805 – 1806	1220. April 2, 1805.
1728	4907	Akshaya ..	982 — 983	1806 – 1807	1221. March 22, 1806.
1729	4908	Prabhava ..	983 — 984	1807 – 1808	1222. March 11, 1807.
1730	4909	Vibhava	984 — 985	1808 – 1809	1223. Feb. 29, 1808.
1731	4910	Śukla	985 — 986	1809 – 1810	1224. Feb. 17, 1809.
1732	4911	Pramodūta ..	986 — 987	1810 – 1811	1225. Feb. 6, 1810.
1733	4912	Prajotpatti ..	987 — 988	1811 – 1812	1226. Jan. 27, 1811.
1734	4913	Āṅgirasa ..	988 — 989	1812 – 1813	1227. Jan. 16, 1812.
1735	4914	Śrīmukha ..	989 — 990	1813 – 1814	1228. Jan. 5, 1813.
1736	4915	Bhava	990 — 991	1814 – 1815	1229. Dec. 25, 1813. 1230. Dec. 14, 1814.
1737	4916	Yuva	991 — 992	1815 – 1816	1231. Dec. 3, 1815.
1738	4917	Dhātu	992 — 993	1816 – 1817	1232. Nov. 21, 1816.
1739	4918	Īśvara	993 — 994	1817 – 1818	1233. Nov. 11, 1817.
1740	4919	Bahudhānya ..	994 — 995	1818 – 1819	1234. Nov. 1, 1818.
1741	4920	Pramādhi ..	995 — 996	1819 – 1820	1235. Oct. 21, 1819.
1742	4921	Vikrama ..	996 — 997	1820 – 1821	1236. Oct. 9, 1820.
1743	4922	Vishu, or Vṛishu.	997 — 998	1821 – 1822	1237. Sept. 28, 1821.
1744	4923	Chitrabhānu ..	998 — 999	1822 – 1823	1238. Sept. 17, 1822.
1745	4924	Subhānu	999 — 1000	1823 – 1824	1239. Sept. 7, 1823.
1746	4925	Tāraṇa	1000 — 1001	1824 – 1825	1240. Aug. 27, 1824.
1747	4926	Pārthiva	1001 — 1002	1825 – 1826	1241. Aug. 16, 1825.
1748	4927	Vyaya	1002 — 1003	1826 – 1827	1242. Aug. 6, 1826.
1749	4928	Sarvajit ..	1003 — 1004	1827 – 1828	1243. July 26, 1827.
1750	4929	Sarvadhāri ..	1004 — 1005	1828 – 1829	1244. July 14, 1828.
1751	4930	Virodhi	1005 — 1006	1829 – 1830	1245. July 3, 1829.

Year of the *Śālivāhana Śaka.*	Year of the *Kaliyuga.*	Cyclic Year.	*Kollaṁ Āṇḍu*, or Era of Quilon.	Christian Era (A.D.)	The *Hijra* Year commences.
1752	4931	Vikṛiti	1006 — 1007	1830 — 1831	1246. June 23, 1830.
1753	4932	Khara	1007 — 1008	1831 — 1832	1247. June 11, 1831.
1754	4933	Nandana ..	1008 — 1009	1832 — 1833	1248. June 1, 1832.
1755	4934	Vijaya	1009 — 1010	1833 — 1834	1249. May 22, 1833.
1756	4935	Jaya	1010 — 1011	1834 — 1835	1250. May 11, 1834.
1757	4936	Manmadha ..	1011 — 1012	1835 — 1836	1251. April 30, 1835.
1758	4937	Durmukhi ..	1012 — 1013	1836 — 1837	1252. April 18, 1836.
1759	4938	Hevilaṁbi ..	1013 — 1014	1837 — 1838	1253. April 7, 1837.
1760	4939	Vilaṁbi	1014 — 1015	1838 — 1839	1254. March 28, 1838.
1761	4940	Vikāri	1015 — 1016	1839 — 1840	1255. March 17, 1839.
1762	4941	Śārvari	1016 — 1017	1840 — 1841	1256. March 6, 1840.
1763	4942	Plava	1017 — 1018	1841 — 1842	1257. Feb. 23, 1841.
1764	4943	Śubhakṛit ..	1018 — 1019	1842 — 1843	1258. Feb. 13, 1842.
1765	4944	Śobhana, or -kṛit,	1019 — 1020	1843 — 1844	1259. Feb. 1, 1843.
1766	4945	Krodhi	1020 — 1021	1844 — 1845	1260. Jan. 22, 1844.
1767	4946	Viśvāvasu ..	1021 — 1022	1845 — 1846	1261. Jan. 10, 1845.
1768	4947	Parābhava ..	1022 — 1023	1846 — 1847	1262. Dec. 31, 1845. 1263. Dec. 20, 1846.
1769	4948	Plavaṅga ..	1023 — 1024	1847 — 1848	1264. Dec. 10, 1847.
1770	4949	Kīlaka	1024 — 1025	1848 — 1849	1265. Nov. 28, 1848.
1771	4950	Saumya	1025 — 1026	1849 — 1850	1266. Nov. 17, 1849.
1772	4951	Sādhāraṇa ..	1026 — 1027	1850 — 1851	1267. Nov. 6, 1850.
1773	4952	Virodhikṛit ..	1027 — 1028	1851 — 1852	1268. Oct. 27, 1851.
1774	4953	Parīdhāvi, or -pi,	1028 — 1029	1852 — 1853	1269. Oct. 15, 1852.
1775	4954	Pramādīcha ..	1029 — 1030	1853 — 1854	1270. Oct. 4, 1853.
1776	4955	Ānanda	1030 — 1031	1854 — 1855	1271. Sept. 24, 1854.
1777	4956	Rākshasa ..	1031 — 1032	1855 — 1856	1272. Sept. 14, 1855.
1778	4957	Nala	1032 — 1033	1856 — 1857	1273. Sept. 1, 1856.
1779	4958	Piṅgala	1033 — 1034	1857 — 1858	1274. Aug. 22, 1857.
1780	4959	Kālayukti ..	1034 — 1035	1858 — 1859	1275. Aug. 11, 1858.
1781	4960	Siddhārthi ..	1035 — 1036	1859 — 1860	1276. Aug. 1, 1859.
1782	4961	Raudri	1036 — 1037	1860 — 1861	1277. July 20, 1860.
1783	4962	Durmati	1037 — 1038	1861 — 1862	1278. July 10, 1861.
1784	4963	Dundubhi ..	1038 — 1039	1862 — 1863	1279. June 29, 1862.
1785	4964	Rudhirodgāri ..	1039 — 1040	1863 — 1864	1280. June 18, 1863.
1786	4965	Raktākshi ..	1040 — 1041	1864 — 1865	1281. June 6, 1864.
1787	4966	Krodhana ..	1041 — 1042	1865 — 1866	1282. May 27, 1865.
1788	4967	Akshaya	1042 — 1043	1866 — 1867	1283. May 16, 1866.
1789	4968	Prabhava ..	1043 — 1044	1867 — 1868	1284. May 5, 1867.

Year of the *Sálivdhana Śaka*.	Year of the *Kaliyuga*.	Cyclic Year.	*Kollam Āndu*, or Era of Quilon.	Christian Era (A.D.)	The *Hijra* Year commences.
1790	4969	Vibhava ..	1044 — 1045	1868 – 1869	1285. April 24, 1868.
1791	4970	Śukla	1045 — 1046	1869 – 1870	1286. April 13, 1869.
1792	4971	Pramodūta ..	1046 — 1047	1870 – 1871	1287. April 3, 1870.
1793	4972	Prajotpatti ..	1047 — 1048	1871 – 1872	1288. March 23, 1871.
1794	4973	Āṅgirasa ..	1048 — 1049	1872 – 1873	1289. March 11, 1872.
1795	4974	Śrīmukha ..	1049 — 1050	1873 – 1874	1290. March 1, 1873.
1796	4975	Bhava	1050 — 1051	1874 – 1875	1291. Feb. 18, 1874.
1797	4976	Yuva	1051 — 1052	1875 – 1876	1292. Feb. 6, 1875.
1798	4977	Dhātu	1052 — 1053	1876 – 1877	1293. Jan. 28, 1876.
1799	4978	Īśvara	1053 — 1054	1877 – 1878	1294. Jan. 16, 1877.
1800	4979	Bahudhānya ..	1054 — 1055	1878 – 1879	1295. Jan. 5, 1878.
1801	4980	Pramādhi ..	1055 — 1056	1879 – 1880	1296. Dec. 26, 1878. 1297. Dec. 15, 1879.
1802	4981	Vikrama	1056 — 1057	1880 – 1881	1298. Dec. 4, 1880.
1803	4982	Vishu, or Vṛishu.	1057 — 1058	1881 – 1882	1299. Nov. 23, 1881.
1804	4983	Chitrabhānu ..	1058 — 1059	1882 – 1883	1300. Nov. 12, 1882.
1805	4984	Subhānu	1059 — 1060	1883 – 1884	1301. Nov. 2, 1883.
1806	4985	Tāraṇa	1060 — 1061	1884 – 1885	1302. Oct. 21, 1884.
1807	4986	Pārthiva	1061 — 1062	1885 – 1886	1303. Oct. 10, 1885.
1808	4987	Vyaya	1062 — 1063	1886 – 1887	1304. Sept. 30, 1886.
1809	4988	Sarvajit	1063 — 1064	1887 – 1888	1305. Sept. 19, 1887.
1810	4989	Sarvadhāri ..	1064 — 1065	1888 – 1889	1306. Sept. 7, 1888.
1811	4990	Virodhi	1065 — 1066	1889 – 1890	1307. Aug. 28, 1889.
1812	4991	Vikṛiti	1066 — 1067	1890 – 1891	1308. Aug. 17, 1890.
1813	4992	Khara	1067 — 1068	1891 – 1892	1309. Aug. 7, 1891.
1814	4993	Nandana ..	1068 — 1069	1892 – 1893	1310. July 26, 1892.
1815	4994	Vijaya	1069 — 1070	1893 – 1894	1311. July 15, 1893.
1816	4995	Jaya	1070 — 1071	1894 – 1895	1312. July 5, 1894.
1817	4996	Manmadha ..	1071 — 1072	1895 – 1896	1313. June 24, 1895.
1818	4997	Durmukhi ..	1072 — 1073	1896 – 1897	1314. June 12, 1896.
1819	4998	Hevilaṁbi ..	1073 — 1074	1897 – 1898	1315. June 2, 1897.
1820	4999	Vilaṁbi	1074 — 1075	1898 – 1899	1316. May 22, 1898.
1821	5000	Vikāri	1075 — 1076	1899 – 1900	1317. May 12, 1899.
1822	5001	Śārvari	1076 — 1077	1900 – 1901	1318. May 1, 1900.

R. S.

SEWELL'S CHRONOLOGICAL TABLES.

(NOTE—*to be kindly inserted.*)

A WORD of warning is necessary for the guidance of those desirous of using these tables. It must be remembered that they were drawn up mainly for the use of those at work on inscriptions and historical documents; and the system adopted has been that of Prinsep, from whose "*Indian Antiquities*" (*Useful Tables*, p. 179,) the following note is extracted:—

"It should be borne in mind that the natives, in speaking or writing a date in simple years, always express the number of years *expired*, not the current year, as is the custom in Europe. When they mention the month, therefore, they mean the month of the following current year: but as the numerical denomination of the Hindú year remains unchanged throughout it, no thought need be taken of the distinction of *expired* years, unless where a calculation has to be made from an initial epoch. In common parlance they may be treated like the current years of any other system, as being more consonant with our ideas and less liable to cause mistakes in transferring dates to and fro."

In using these tables, therefore, it must be remembered that the *Ś. Śaka* and *Kaliyuga* years entered against the name of any particular cyclic year are the years whose numerical denomination is actually used in documents throughout that year, but that the real astronomical number is the one next following.

Thus; for the current year, *Chitrabhānu* (1882-1883), all documents would bear the *Śaka* number 1804, and the *Kaliyuga* 4983, but actually the current *Śaka* is 1805 and the *Kaliyuga* 4984. The expression used in documents would be "*Śaka* 1804 having expired," or "following on *Śaka* 1804."

R. SEWELL.

MADRAS, *April* 1882.

Published by

Facsimile Publisher
Ashok Vihar, Delhi-110052 (India)
Website: www.facsimilepublisher.com

Distributed by

Gyan Books Pvt. Ltd.
5, Ansari Road, Daryaganj, New Delhi-110002 (India)
E-mail: books@gyanbooks.com, Website: www.gyanbooks.com

2 222000 000387